Dedicated to my son

Henry,

with love,

as he heads off

to Bath.

INTRODUCTION

Civil Litigation, Evidence and Remedies is possibly the most challenging part of the Bar Professional Training Course for many students. It is also a topic were, if you can grasp the key concepts early and drill down and memorise the detail, it is possible to score highly and enjoy this fascinating area of law. This book assumes the reader has completed LLB or GDL successfully. This book is not intended to be a beautiful piece of prose. It seeks to avoid long winded narrative and instead distils the syllabus into bullet points that are easy to read and remember. The aim is to help students achieve a strong understanding early. Its purpose is to make civil litigation easier and more fun to understand.

This book is based on the structure of the BPTC syllabus and will be updated as the syllabus evolves over time. It is definitely not to be read instead of the practitioner text or textbook. It should significantly help with revision.

A GUIDE TO USING THIS BOOK

It can be helpful to use revision books continuously over time to support early progress and make subjects easier and more fun to understand, but definitely not instead of your practitioner text or textbook. The list at Chapter 24 is not a BSB list but may serve as a helpful checklist of things you might aim to be able to recite in full by the end of your BPTC year.

It is also important to refer to the syllabus for the relevant authorities. Aspects of the syllabus change from time to time and by referring to the BSB website you can be sure but that you are using the latest version. Abbreviations and references to statute and the civil procedure rules are identified by [square brackets]. It is important that each original reference is referred to at the same time whilst using this book, use your practitioner text. Important cases are referred to in the body of the text.

You might consider downloading the program ANKI, which is free online, or costs a small amount to download to your phone. Make multiple choice style flashcards of the CPR. That way you can flick through them on your phone whilst on the train etc. You can get a lot done this way.

Work hard. Seize the day. Approach BPTC rather like training for a long run. Do a little and often. Keep going, invest in practice continuously over time, taking things gradually at first. Be sure that practice does pay off. Invest the time you need to do well.

Good luck.

SJ Woodall
August 2016

ABOUT THE AUTHOR

SJ Woodall is a Visiting Professor at the Dickinson Poon School of Law at King's College London. She initially read psychology and, after joining the British Civil Service via its fast stream, worked as a Senior Civil Servant in the British Government in Westminster. Specialising in tax law, Sarah headed up criminal prosecution for the Inland Revenue and was later head of anti-avoidance investigation for HMRC. Having always been bit in awe of the advocacy skills of counsel she had instructed over the years, SJ Woodall took courage after winning Middle Temple's Harmsworth Scholarship and finally decided to qualify as a barrister for herself.

COMMON ABBREVIATIONS

In the spirit of revision notes and to keep this text short, abbreviations are used throughout this book. The abbreviations most commonly used are:

<	Less than
>	More Than
A	Appellant
ADR	Alternate Dispute Resolution
ATE	After the Event Insurance
BPTC	Bar Professional Training Course
C	Claimant
CC	County Court / Counterclaim, *according to context*
CFA	Conditional Fee Arrangement
CJEU	Court of Justice of the European Union
CofA	Court of Appeal
CMC	Case Management Conference
CMR	Cost Management Regime
CPR	Civil Procedure Rules
D	Defendant
DBA	Damages Based Agreement
DJ	Default Judgement
ECHR	European Court of Human Rights
HC	High Court
LAA	Legal Aid Agency
LP	Legal Privilege
LPP	Legal Professional Privilege
P/s	Party
Para/s	Paragraph/s

PD	Practice Direction
PI	Personal Injuries
PII	Public Interest Immunity
PSLA	Pain, Suffering and Loss of Amenity
R	Respondent
r/R	Rule/s
re	Regarding
s/Ss	Section/s
W	Witness
WS	Witness Statement

All errors in this book remains the author's own. Every effort has been made to state the law as applicable as at 3 August 2016.

***

TABLE OF CONTENTS

CHAPTER 1

Allocation of cases; HC and CC - CPR rules and PD 7A

Only 1 HC and 1 CC (both single courts and both Senior Courts), in multiple locations.

- CC hears the most straightforward and lower value cases
- <u>Some cases only start in CC:</u>
  - landlord and tenant;
  - consumer credit agreements;
  - PI claims less than **< £50 K;**
  - non-PI claims of **£100k, or less;**
- <u>Some claims only start HC:</u>
  - JR;
  - contentious probate;
  - slander, libel;
  - damages re judicial acts under HRA 1998.
- HC deals with more important and complex civil cases and is divided into 3 divisions:
  - Chancery Division; land, trust and probate;
  - Family Division;
  - Queen's Bench Division(QBD); most tort and contract cases; includes administrative court that hears JR
- Where both HC / CC have jurisdiction, a case can start in either. Factors to consider are:
  - value;
  - complexity – of fact or law;
  - public importance.

1.1— Overriding Objective [OO]

1) new procedural code; overriding objective of enabling court deal with cases **justly** and at **proportionate cost.**

2) includes

a) ensuring Ps on equal footing;

b) saving expense;

c) dw case proportionate to—

i. money;

ii. importance;

iii. complexity; and

iv. financial position of each P;

e) ensure dw expeditiously and fairly;

f) allotting appropriate share of court resources, taking into account needs of other cases; and

g) enforcing compliance with rules, PDs and orders.

1.2 - Application - forces court to weigh issues of procedural **justice** and **proportionate cost** in

a) exercises of any power given by Rules; or

b) when interprets Rules,

1.3 - Duty of Ps; to help court further OO.

1.4—Court's duty to manage cases actively to further overriding objective

1) court must further OO by **actively managing cases**.

2) Active case management includes:

a) encouraging Ps to co-operate

b) identifying issues early

c) deciding promptly which issues need full investigation and trial, dispose summarily of others;

d) deciding order issues resolved in;

e) encouraging use of ADR and **facilitating use** of ADR;

f) helping Ps settle whole or part of case;

g) fixing timetables or controlling progress of case;

h) considering whether benefits of a step justify cost;

i) dw as many aspects of case as possible on same occasion;
j) dw case without Ps needing to attend court;
k) making use of technology;
l) giving **directions** to ensure trial proceeds quickly and efficiently.

- Overriding objective does not override specific CPR rules but can come into play when deciding how to;
  - apply; or
  - exercise discretion granted by a rule.
- Mitchell v Sun Newspaper; example of how relatively minor breach of rules can lead to major consequences
  - Solicitor provided costs budget per **CPR 3.12** a bit late;
  - did not escape sanctions under **CPR 3.14** and costs recovered were limited to court costs;
  - illustrates real emphasis or determination by Court on developing a culture of enforced compliance.

Article 6 ECHR ;
- Provides that the Courts' strict approach to sanctions under CPR likely to be acceptable provided can show:
  - pursuing a legitimate aim; and
  - sanctions are proportionate to breach.
- Court must further overriding objective by active case management
  - often involves court **directions** at case management conferences:
  - after application; or
  - of own motion;
  - Court may do so at any time.

Active case management includes promoting:
- cooperation;
- ADR;
- early identification issues; and
- fixing timetables;
- dealing with case without parties attending; and
- giving directions to ensure trial proceeds quickly.

***

CHAPTER 2

Limitation.

- Ethos of CPR is that litigation is to be avoided where possible through:
  - ADR;
  - cost disincentives;
  - pre-action conduct;
- if litigation becomes necessary it should be commenced promptly with the limitation period;
- amendments made late will only exceptionally be allowed once limitation period has expired;
- effective case management by Court is vital to force pace of litigation.
- Limitation Act 1980; gives certainty.
- Underlying principle: not good for society for claims to hang around.
- It would be hard on defendants if they were perpetually at risk of being sued:
  - memories become vague;
  - evidence can degrade;
  - purpose of limitation period is to limit time during which action can be successfully pursued.

- "Time-barred" is misleading as limitation rules do not kill substantive course of action
- Limitation are rules of procedure not substantive law and offer D scope to stay claim on procedural grounds:
  - C can still issue claim in civil court after limitation period;
  - 'limitation period' is date beyond which C cannot be granted a remedy;

- if C continues an action which is time-barred, D can apply to have case struck out as an abuse of process
- procedural defence; bars the right to remedy not the right to bring claim.

"expiry of limitation period bars the remedy [e.g. damages] not the right"

Defence of limitation must be raised by D:
- Defence of limitation must be raised by D,
- it is a complete defence:
- Court will not raise on own initiative;
- will not be anticipated in Cs' particulars of claim;
- claim can be started on last day of limitation period;
- **accrual** = date cause of action arises / limitation starts
- Limitation period runs out after time specified by Limitation Act 1980;
- can stop limitation period expiring by **bringing proceedings** as then the limitation **clock stops.**
- If court closed on final day, in time if received next working day.
Proceedings brought:
- proceedings are brought when claim form and payment **delivered to court by C (this is date issued)**;
  - 3rd party claims deemed to commence on date third party/ Part 20 claim form issued (see chapter 5);
  - even if court did not issue claim form until after time has lapsed;
  - counterclaims and set off deemed to commence on same date as original action; backdated to that date;
  - counter claim can be made at any time so long as claim it relates to was made in time.
- Time runs from first full day after date cause of action accrues;
  - do not count day on which cause of action accrued, count from next day

[if breach on 1 January 2015, time starts on 2 January + 6 yrs. Say limitation period "runs out on 1 January 2021", but can still can bring proceedings that day];

- **Do say** *correct term; discretion to* **disapply** *limitation provisions [s33LA];*
- **Do not say***; discretion to override time-limit*

Differences between contract and tort:

- **Contract**: any breach actionable and cause of action accrues date of breach;
- most **torts** require **damage to be actionable** - time begins at **time of damage** for tort of negligence [some torts are actionable without proof of damage].

Type of action	Limitation Period [LP]	Limitation Act [LA]
Tort	**6 yrs.** Time runs from date tort committed, if actionable per se or [*most tort actions actionable only on proof of damage then time runs from]* date of damage	S2 LA
Contract	**6 yrs.** Time runs from date of breach	S5 LA - [LP Final, cannot be disapplied]

PI / fatal accident	3 yrs.	S11
for LA *Includes any disease or impairment of a person's physical or mental condition*	Time runs from date action accrues or if claimant does not realise he has been injured, from date of knowledge	S14 Definition date of knowledge for s11 and 12., from date of injury or death or date of knowledge, if later Date of knowledge is first date C knew all of [3]: injuries sufficiently serious to justify commencing proceedings; caused by alleged act or omission; identity of D or where act/ omission not of D but of 3rdP (vicarious liability), identity of 3rdP Knowledge of law is irrelevant **Knowledge[1] includes:** **Actual knowledge;** and **Constructive knowledge**; C might reasonably be expected to acquire including by consulting experts or lawyer. Not fixed with knowledge if expert got it wrong e.g. said C not ill.

---

[1] Date of knowledge provisions introduced in 1960s to assist miners with damaged lungs who were often unaware of injuries for years.
Some litigants still failed to bring claim once they had the requisite knowledge; sometimes employers had given bad advice.
 S 33 LA 1980 gives court discretion where it thinks it equitable; to let a personal injury action proceed notwithstanding it is out of time.
Court does not extend the limitation period rather overlooks that it has expired; called disapplying the limitation period.
 Section 33 (3); the court should have regards to all the circumstances of the case when deciding whether to exercise discretion
 In particular factors listed at section 33 (3) (a)-(f); the list is not exhaustive.

S 33 LA 1980 PI/ FA	Extends 3+	S33
court discretion where it thinks it is equitable; to let PI actions proceed notwithstanding it is out of time.	In PI / FA cases only	Court's discretion to extend 3yrs considering: length and reason for delay by C; damage to cogency of evidence (of C or D); D's conduct after cause of action arose; re reasonable requests; duration of disability of C, after date of accrual; extent C acted promptly and reasonably once aware act or omission of D may be capable of giving rise to action; steps taken by C to obtain medical, legal, expert advice and nature such advice.
Latent damage negligence (Injury to buildings etc. rather than injured people.)	**6 years+** or 3 years from date of knowledge **15yr longstop**	**Latent damage = hidden damage** [injury to buildings etc. not people[2]] applies only to negligence, all other torts excluded; never PI / fatal accident. **S 14A** LA, limitation negligence later of: 6 yrs. from date of accrual (normal); 3 yrs. from date of knowledge Definition of knowledge; same as for PI **S 14B Longstop** [on latent damage in negligence claims only] 15 yr. long stop from date of act / omission alleged to be negligent Called overriding time-limit

---

[2] Latent Damage Act 1986. Sometimes damage for example to buildings happens before it is noticeable. Where damage other than personal injuries is latent, not patent, claim in tort of negligence maybe brought under this Act; inserted in s14A and 14B LA.

Two important differences between latent damage and personal injuries:
* long stop; prevents latent damage cases being brought after 15 years from negligent act;
* no discretion to disapply relevant limitation period as there is in PI cases.

		Longstop does not apply in cases of fraud, deliberate concealment or mistake.
Fraud / deliberate concealment / mistake	Postpones start date available under S 32	<u>S 32 LA; -</u> **Fraud**; time does not begin to run until C: Discovers; or could reasonably have discovered **fraud.** **Relevant fact deliberately concealed;** time not run until C: discovers; or could reasonably have discovered **concealment.** <u>Fact concealed must be one D:</u> has duty to disclose; or would have disclosed in normal course of relationship but D decided not to disclose. **Mistake:** time does not run until C: discovers; or could "<u>with reasonable diligence</u>" have discovered mistake. Mistake must be **essential element** of cause of action E.g. money paid in consequence of the mistake - mistake of fact or law.
Children And Protected parties[3]	LP does not begin to run	**S 28** Disability does not mean physical disability, refers to: Children (Under 18); or protected parties; those

---

[3] A person who has not yet attained age of majority said to be acting under a disability. So is a protected person who lacks mental capacity to conduct proceedings. If at the time action would otherwise have arisen C is under 18 or of unsound mind, time will not begin to run until mental capacity has ended, or C achieves age of 18. Once time limit has started to run later mental incapacity cannot stop it again.

		unable to make decisions for self because impairment in functioning of mind or brain Time; does not begin until party <u>no longer under a disability</u>
Contribution claims under Civil Liability (Contribution) Act 1978	**2 years**	**S 10 (1)** – no action to recover a contribution shall be brought **2 years** after accrual date. **Accrual date is:** if P liable for damage: date of judgment on liability; or date of arbitration award no account taken of any judgment or award given or made on appeal if appeal only varies amount of damages. If P not liable but agrees to compensate one or more Ps for damage, accrual date is **earliest date on which amount paid is agreed** between him and P to whom damages awarded.

***

CHAPTER 3

Pre-action Conduct

- CPR introduced a formal system for early exchange information intended to increase opportunity for settlement **without proceedings being issued**. It did this via:
  - Pre-action protocols, tailored to different types of dispute; and
  - Practice Direction: Pre-action Conduct [PD-PAC] governing pre-action behavior in cases not covered by existing protocol.
- 2 main pre-action conduct objectives are:
  - empower Ps to resolve disputes fairly at proportionate cost without starting proceedings; and
  - where court proceedings cannot be avoided, ensure cases proceeds efficiently.

Four elements to typical pre-action protocol:
1. **Letter before claim [LBC]:**
- Sending this letter starts formal pre-action process;
- concise and includes sufficient detail so D can understand and investigate without asking for more information;
- should contain, and seek from D, any relevant documents key to disputed issues;
- should be professional, not spiteful;
- should inform D of funding arrangements which will impact on them, if C is publicly funded or insured.

2. **Prompt identification of issues**
- Typically, a protocol requires <u>D to respond within reasonable time</u>; varies according to complexity from:
  - **14 days** in simple case; to
  - no more than **3 months** in complex case.
- In responding D should:
- confirm accepted aspects of claim, and

- provide C with documentary evidence and/or explanation for any denial of liability,
- make clear if contributory negligence is alleged; or
- if D intends to counterclaim.
- Aim is: each side understands other's position and can make informed decision about what to do.

3. Early exchange of relevant evidence:
- Relevant documents are exchanged almost from outset;
- Aim is; both sides should be in position to assess strength of their respective cases;
- expert evidence can be crucial but can only be relied on <u>if Court gives permission</u> (see chapter 19).
- Various protocols differ in their requirements
- Reducing costs is the aim of the generic PD PAC.
- An important way expense saved is by use of single expert which can be agreed in a number of ways;

1. **Jointly agreed and selected [JAS]:** one side pays, gives instructions, calls expert evidence and retains LPP of the evidence until and unless disclosed to other side.
or
2. **Jointly instructed [JI]:** both parties participate in selection of and instruct the expert, who sends a copy of report to both. Generally, costs shared. This is the norm in fast-track cases
or
3. **One party could get expert evidence independently [I]:** and hope its use can be agreed by the Court (tends to arise with medical evidence where patient seeks medical opinion from his own doctor in the process of formulating a cause of action).

- PD-PAC reminds Ps, many disputes can be resolved without expert evidence and if it is necessary, a jointly instructed single expert is to be preferred.

4. Importance of ADR

- Protocols and PD-PAC all reinforce message; litigation should be last resort and stress importance of:
  - reality checks;
  - continual thoughts re alternative ways to resolve dispute, even after proceedings have started.
- In most cases court will want to know what steps Ps are taking to settle.
- Sir Rupert Jackson: aim is "*no case should come to trial without Ps undertaking some form of ADR to settle case*":
  - duty is to consider ADR;
  - not necessarily to engage in ADR;
  - not all cases are suited to ADR.

Compliance and proportionality:

- Compliance with pre-action conduct taken very seriously;
- important to approach protocol in right spirit, not to gain unfair advantage.
- Potential sanctions for willful non-compliance:
  - court may not extend time limits; or
  - adverse costs order may be awarded.
- Only reasonable and proportionate steps should be taken during pre-action phase:
- disproportionate costs may not be recovered.
- Circumstances may justify departure from the protocol particularly if mediation taking place.
- Any punishment for non-compliance should be in keeping with the overriding objective.
  [Now read PDP AC paragraph 1-17]

S I I I – PD- PAC:

- cases not covered by published protocol must comply with ethos of PD-PAC; and
- in accordance with the overriding objective, reasonably exchange info and documents relevant to claim; and
- try to avoid court proceedings

Order of key events for PD-PAC:

Step	Comment
C sends D **Letter Before Claim** **[LBC]**	Detailed letter. Sets out; facts: basis of claim: docs C relies on
Conditional fee agreement [CFA or ATE]	If C or D has CFA or ATE[4] insurance must notify other side immediately
D has reasonable time to reply	Depends on case; from 14 to 90 days, according to complexity
D's replies	**Must indicate whether liability accepted in full, part or denied**
Preliminary exchange of docs	Both C and D may ask other for Copies of relevant documents **Note:** use of docs limited to resolution of this dispute
Negotiation / ADR	C and D must consider negotiation/ ADR and retain evidence that it was considered

Non-compliance with pre-action protocols and PD-PAC:
- although not officially binding, as set out best practice, deliberate non-compliance may result in court sanction.
- Non-compliance with PAP may be justified in some circumstances:
  - e.g. if issuing proceedings before negotiations are finished to prevent being time-barred; then no sanction
- **If court decides on sanction it may:**
  - order stay - to allow compliance;
  - make costs order - on defaulting P;

---

[4] *Conditional fee arrangement / After the Event Insurance*

- order costs on indemnity basis;
- If C at fault and eventually wins, <u>deprive C of interest</u> or decrease normal rate;
- if D at fault and eventually loses, award interest at <u>higher rate;</u>
- defaulting P may be ordered to <u>pay money in to court</u>, if default without good reason.

***

CHAPTER 4

Commencing Proceedings.

- CPR introduced single **code of practice**; applies to all civil court but some specialist areas excluded e.g. family law.
- Proceedings begin when C issues claim form at Court and pays Court fee;
- Court issues claim form by adding Court number and Court seal; it is now ready to be served.
- Generally, any document prepared or issued by Court, including claim form, will be served by Court
- C may notify Court of wish to serve claim form himself.
- Where a P brings a civil action will depend on rules about:
    - jurisdiction; which court is capable of dealing with the claim; and
    - commencement; where to start a claim.
  [Important not to confuse 2 concepts]

Jurisdiction:
- Cases where only CC has **jurisdiction**:
    - unlawful discrimination;
    - lower value consumer credit claims
      Cases were only HC has **jurisdiction:**
    - libel
    - JR;
    - equity cases exceeding >£350,000.
- In majority of contract and tort cases, HC and CC have **concurrent jurisdiction**; either has power to deal with case.

Rules about Commencement
- Although jurisdiction concurrent, commencement rules dictate where actions **must start:**
- Must commence in CC if:
    - seeking damages in PI and FA claims of <u>less than</u> < £50,000:
    - amount sought must amount C reasonably expects to recover

[*when calculating claim disregard: costs; interest; contributory negligence*];
- other types of money claims <u>not exceeding £100,000.</u>
• These rules are about commencement, not jurisdiction; they force C to begin smaller cases in CC.
• There are possible sanctions for non-compliance with commencement rules:
  - claim may be struck out; or
  - a penalty in costs at end of trial or when case transferred between courts.
• <u>It does not follow that claims crossing threshold must be started in HC:</u>
• where C believes HC could better deal with claim because of its:
  - complexity; or
  - public importance;
○ case should be started in HC;
• same factors also dictate where claims to remedies other than money should be commenced; injunctions etc.;
• as part of its case management powers, Court can transfer cases between HC and CC for same reasons either on:
  - own initiative; or
  - application by any P.
• Where case may ultimately be tried is another factor which influences where C with choice decides to start action.

How to start Proceedings – normally Part 7
• **Civil** proceedings involving <u>normal factual disputes</u> start by issue of <u>Part 7</u> claim form;
  - negligence, breach-of-contract, breach of trust.
• claim form issued by Court at C's request;
• it need not set out all specifics of case as this is done in Particulars of Claim which sets out (PABLIR- Parties, Agreement, Breach, Loss, Interest, Remedy):
  - cause of action;
  - facts;
  - remedy sought;

- in PI actions a medical report, <u>schedule of past and future loss</u> and expense accompanies Particulars of Claim.

Particulars of Claim can either be:

- contained in Part 7 claim form; or
- attached to Part 7 claim form; or
- follow within 14 days of service of claim form.
- Where Particulars of Claim not attached because draft is too long or time short, claim form must give details of:

1. nature of claim;
2. remedy sort;
3. the response pack; forms for defending / admitting claim and acknowledgement of service;

- when money at stake contain a statement of value for track allocation purposes
  - Less than £10,000;
  - £10,000- £25,000;
  - more than £25,000; or
  - don't know
- If commenced in HC, Part 7 claim must state relevant threshold has been crossed or this is specialist HC case.
- If Particulars of Claim is not contained in it, Part 7 Claim Form should state whether is attached or to follow.
- Claim form must contain statement of truth.
- If served separately, a copy of Particulars of Claim and <u>Certificate of Service</u> must be filed with the court.

Not all disputes are fact based – Part 8:

- Disputes about <u>legal questions or issues</u> are initiated using Part 8 Claim Form;
- typically, such cases may involve:
  - no substantial dispute of fact;
  - approval of settlements by / against a child;
  - trustee seeking court guidance;
  - Court construing a document such as will or deed;
  - a requirement to use Part 8 by rule or PD.

- <u>Written evidence is served</u> with Part 8 claim form, not a Particulars of Claim;
- any trial involves legal submissions on the evidence, not cross-examination of witness
- <u>In general:</u>
  - where no claim brought but issue requires judge's determination, Part 8 is mechanism to use;
  - majority of claims are fact based Part 7 claims, and for money;
  - money only claims in CC should be sent to Money Claims Centre, Salford;
  - C indicates on form which hearing center C prefers and undefended cases sent there;
  - defended cases tend to go to Ds preferred or local hearing center, but not usually referred until after directions questionnaires have been filed.

Responding to Part 8 claim; D acknowledges service stating:
  - whether contests claim;
  - whether seeking different remedy; and
  - if D thinks Part 8 should not be used, why not.

Summary re issue of Claim form:
- an action commences when claim form issued (not served);
- claim form must be served on a D whilst it is still valid;
- claim form is valid for **4 months**; time runs from <u>day after</u> claim form is issued
  [*D does not need to receive claim form during period of validity*];
- extending period of validity of claim form is called renewal, rather like renewing library book.

Statements of case should be titled and state:
  - number of proceedings;
  - court or division of proceedings;
  - full name each P;
  - status of each P (Claimant, Defendant, 3rd-P etc.);
  - must be served on D with particulars of claim **within 4 months** of issuing.

Court discretion to extend time limit for service of claim form where:

- C acted promptly; and
- court failed to serve claim form; or
- C took all reasonable steps to serve, but not been able to;
- extension may be granted with consent of
  - P to be served; or
  - Court.

Application to renew if limitation period has not yet expired

- an alternative to renewal is to **issue fresh proceedings;**
- renewal typically sought where C is having difficulties serving D;
- **general rule:** application for extension of claim form's validity should be made before claim form expires:
- called a prospective application;
- Court has a general discretion to renew and will exercise it:
  - in accordance with the overriding objective;
  - looking at attempts made to serve; and
  - considering the reason for renewal; better the reason the more likely to allow.
- Good reasons include
  - D behaving badly or
  - D evading service.
- if there is good reason Court should consider balance of hardship between Ps; particularly where limitation period has expired
- Court's general approach to renewal is tough:
  - C should issue and serve proceedings promptly
  - this is not difficult.
- The Court has complete discretion.

Application to renew after claim form has expired [CPR 7.6]:

- called retrospective application;
- Court's discretion severely constrained here by CPR 7.6 and C must show:

- has taken all reasonable steps yet failed to serve claim form within 4-months; and

  [note: steps taken after 4-month point are irrelevant]
- application made promptly;
- focus is only on attempts to serve
- CPR 7.6 constitutes a complete code and even overriding objective only mitigates severity of rule in exceptional circumstances including applying retrospectively:
  - for order for <u>alternate service;</u>
  - an order <u>dispensing with service</u>, only granted exceptionally if an attempt has been made to serve;
  - to remedy <u>technical error</u> in service;

Procedure Application for renewal:

- Application for renewal is made to an interim judge under Part 23:
  - using an application notice;
  - supported by evidence;
  - setting out relevant time periods; and
  - reason why renewal is necessary;
  - because there is no D on record, application is made without notice
- D who wishes to dispute extension granted must:
  - acknowledge service stating an intention to defend then;
  - apply on notice **within 7 days of service** to have extending order discharged

    [D must act promptly as delay may be interpreted as acceptance of valid service]
- Rules reflect that Court must be satisfied there was <u>compelling reason</u> for C not doing something as easy as putting a claim form in the post.
- Applications for renewal after both limitation period and claim form have expired will be lost

[Remember: as long as limitation period has not expired, a fresh action can always be started].

Following found insufficient step for extension:
- incompetence or oversight by C;
- serving on D who had nominated a solicitor then failing to serve on solicitor after realising mistake;
- D had not replied to letter of claim;
- report re quantum arrived late;
- difficulty securing ATE insurance for claim.

Six methods of service by C of claim form and other docs

1. **Personal service**, C personally giving D claim form. Not allowed if:
- C brings proceedings against crown
- D represented by solicitor and has supplied solicitor's address*.

2. **Leaving at an address including:**
- D's solicitor's address for service;
- address nominated by D;
- D's last known address, if suspect not current, C must take reasonable steps to find current address and serve there
  (or make application to court to serve by alternative method/ or place)
3. **Contractually agreed method**

4. **By First Class Post or DX**

5. **Electronic method**; fax / email:
- D must have indicated agreement in writing to accept service by fax or email;
- if unrepresented party willingness must be given explicitly - fax number on litigant's notepaper not enough
- where service on P's solicitor, willingness to be served by fax sufficiently indicated by including
- fax number - on headed paper;

- this is not enough for e mail: litigant's solicitor's must
- explicitly state willingness to be served by email and email address on paper may be used for this purpose
  [i.e. e-mail on headed paper, only with express permission];
- putting fax number or email on **statement of case** or **response to claim** is sufficient indication of willingness to be served in that way.

- **Other method authorised by court**

Note: Where Solicitor acting:
- Where C given written notice that:
  - D's solicitor is authorised to accept service; and
  - relevant solicitors' business address has been provided;
- all documents, including claim form, **must** be served at that address.

When did service of claim form occur?
- Strict generic rule: service of claim form **deemed** to take effect on **2nd business day after completion of required step;**
  - even applies to personal service, which is instantaneous;
  - weekends and holidays are not business days;
- Effect of deeming provisions for claim form:
  - service takes effect on deemed date and no other;
  - if post returned, Court notifies C yet claim form still **deemed to be served;**
  - deeming provisions create an irrebuttable presumption of law;
  - advantage of letting courts issue claim form; C does not need to provide certificate of service or prove service.
- Issue by Court is normal method for claim form, by 1st class post;
- C must notify Court if C wishes to serve claim form;

- service by preparing party is normal method of service for balance of documents;
- there is no overarching deeming provision for service of documents other than claim form itself.

Timing of service:

Method of Service	Deemed Served om	CPR
All Claim forms	Deemed served on **2nd business day** after completion of relevant step for service	6.14
All other documents	Examples at PD 6A[10]	
1st class post or DX	**2nd day after posting**, provided that day is a business day (if not, the next business day)	6.26
Fax / e mail / personal service	**Same day**: if before 4:30 on a business day **Next business Day**: if after 4:30	6.26

Place of service depends on status of D:

Serving Defendant who is:	Special Rule must serving Claim Form on
Child, but not a protected party	Claim form must be served on; parents or guardians or (if no such person exists) adults with whom child resides or in whose care child is <u>Once litigation friend identified:</u> Service of <u>all subsequent documents</u> is on litigation friend *[These rules do not apply where Court allows proceedings without litigation friend, CPR 6.13]*
Protected Parties	Claim form must be served on; person with enduring lasting <u>power of attorney</u>; person appointed by court of protection; or adult with whom protected P resides <u>Other documents must be served on litigation friend</u> C may apply to serve on different P.

Partnership	**Court normally uses first class post** to partnership firm address or Other addresses given for service **For C serving claim form himself:** if C notified of solicitors authorised to accept service; C must serve defendant **at solicitor's address**; by post leaving form, DX etc. partnership **can be served personally**; leaving claim form with any partner, or person having control or management of partnership at time of service at principal place of business Service can be affected by post/ leaving/ faxing etc. to **principle or last known place of business of firm or another address provided by D**
Sole trader	At usual or last known residence or his principle or last known place of business
Companies	**Under CPR;** at principal office or any place of business of Co which has real connection with claim or Personal service on <u>senior person</u> in company **Under Companies Act 2006;** At registered office, unless proved to the contrary
Contractually agreed service	Any contractually agreed method of service, if action based solely on the contract
Alternative Service	It is not often that one of available methods of service will not work. If Court persuaded there is a good reason, it can make an order permitting service: by an alternative method; or at an alternative place; application must be supported by <u>written evidence</u> including what is proposed If Court makes an order for alternative service it should also specify: <u>when</u> such service deemed to be served and <u>how long</u> D has to respond Alternatively, Court can order steps C has already taken constitute good service. *[This is an example of interim application which out of necessity made without notice to other side]*
No service	**In exceptional circumstances** court may dispense with need to serve <u>claim form</u>: E.g., where tiny technical fault with service but not possible to try to serve again properly.

	C may make application seeking court exercise such power **at any time**, provided supported by evidence; may be made without notice to prospective D.
	Court may dispense with service of any <u>other document</u> **without exceptional circumstances**.

***

Burden of Proof ∧ (on) whether the representation
was made in a misrepresentation case [~~has~~]
cp to the claimant.

The <u>Reversed Burden of proof</u> under <u>Misrepresentation</u>
<u>Act 1967 S 2(1)</u>

CHAPTER 5

Parties

Children – see also chapter 18.
- Individual attains full age at 18;
- until then considered to be acting **"under a disability"**.
- Children must sue and defend by their litigation friend although;
- court may order a child is able to conduct proceedings without litigation friend.
- **Child remains the party** but must litigate by means of the litigation friend
- Title of proceedings looks like this;

> *Miss HILLARY HOUSE*   ___*Claimant*___
> *(a child by Mr. GEORGE HOUSE, her litigation friend).*

- Most litigation friends are voluntary, appointed without court order;
- typically, child's parent or guardian
- Must be someone with no conflicting interest and if child is C, undertakes to pay costs ordered against child.
- Litigation friend must file a *certificate of suitability* with court
- If no one available, court can order a litigation friend be appointed

Settlements of money claims by a child require special attention because:
- Children need protection from exploitation; and
- Ds need to know settlement is final
- Unless proposed children's settlement is approved by court, there is no binding agreement on either party.
- Court should be asked to approve settlement as being in child's best interests

Procedure for obtaining court approval:

i. <u>If no action started</u>; Part 8 claim form used to seek court approval setting out detail of:
 - claim;
 - proposed settlement;
 - court approval not required by CPR, as case is pre-action, but advisable, or settlement not binding.

ii. <u>Once proceedings commence</u>:
 - to be valid settlement must be approved by Court;
 - Part 7 form will already have been issued, application for approval is **interim application under CPR 23;**
 - Ps can apply for hearing to approve settlement.

- <u>Where money to be paid to child</u> under settlement court normally directs:
 - money paid in to court;
 - invested for benefit of child;
 - paid to child at 18.

Mental incapacity - Protected Persons:

- Persons <u>lacking mental capacity to conduct litigation</u> known as protected parties;
- also treated as persons acting under a disability;
- **must** sue and defend by their litigation friend;
- unlike a child, Court will **never** order a protected P is able to conduct proceedings on own behalf;
- Court approval should be sought for any settlement as above.

Partnerships and sole traders:

- **Partnership** trade under a firm name;
- Typically, each partner bound by acts done on behalf of firm and liable;
- claims by or against partnership must use firm name under which partnership carried on business at time cause of action arose;
- fact it is partnership signified by words **"a firm"** after the name;
  Woodall and Woodall (a firm) **[PAF]**

- **Sole traders** if not trading in own name, **may** be sued in a business name (as if it were a partnership);
- helps C who might not know name of person behind business name;
- title should reflect the status of sole trader for example;
  Bits and Bobs (a trading name) **[STAT]**
- A **trader bringing a claim** knows his own name so is **not given this option and uses his own name.**

Companies

- Limited companies must sue and be sued using registered company name;
- company created to limit liability of owners;
- has its own legal personality.

Bankrupts and dead

- When person becomes bankrupt all causes of action vest in trustee in bankruptcy;
  "the trustee of the estate of Ms. Sarah Woodall, a bankrupt"
- If C becomes bankrupt in course of proceedings, trustee in bankruptcy may carry on if Court agrees to substitute name of trustee.
- Claims involving trust property may be brought by against trustees, without joining beneficiaries.
- Any judgement will bind beneficiaries unless Court orders otherwise
- Claim only ceases on death of C if cause of action is **personal to him;** e.g. libel, defamation;
- otherwise executor's or administrators can take over claim, if Court agrees to substitute their names.
- On death of D, C may apply for an order to continue action against his personal representatives.
- If action commenced against someone dead at time started, treated as if it were brought against estate of deceased.

Charities and trusts:

- Trustees/ Executors/ Administrators- should act jointly;
- all should be named in proceedings;

- claim may be brought by or against:
  - trustees;
  - executors; or
  - administrators;
    - o no need to join beneficiaries.

Joinder of Parties and Causes of Action:

- CPR allows C to join causes of action and/or Ps in one claim form, without seeking permission
- Case management powers mean Court has last word regarding which claims heard together, taking into account overriding objective and the need to:
  - save expenses; and
  - deal with cases expeditiously and fairly.

  ### Joining Causes of Action
  #### By claimant [CPR 7.3]:
- C may use single claim form to start **all claims** which can **"be conveniently disposed of"**[5] in same proceedings;
- no permission necessary;
- Court will ultimately decide whether to hear cases together or not.

  #### By defendant
- D can raise a claim against C by counterclaim; joins cause of action to the one brought against D;
- **no permission** required if counterclaim is against C alone and filed at same time as defence;
- **no connection** between claim and counterclaim required although;
- if completely unrelated, Court may separate it.

  ### Joining Parties
  #### By claimant
- CPR 19.1 says **any number** of Cs and Ds may be joined as Ps to claim;

---

[5] CPR 7.3

- In conjunction with CPR 7.3 this gives C freedom when starting claims which can be "conveniently disposed of" on one claim form, to join as many Ps to Claim as relevant
- **"Convenience"** requires a degree of **interrelationship between parties and claims**
By defendant
- **Ds can bring parties into proceedings in 2 ways:**
  - if **counterclaiming**; can **join co-Ds** to counterclaim, **with permission** of court
  - D can bring in third parties, another form of additional claim
- Court is ultimate arbiter of what is convenient to be disposed of together;
- will order separate trial whenever it believes this will further the overriding objective.
- Where 2 actions, Court also has power to order consolidated into single action, if would further overriding objective
- Court also has wide discretion to remove add or substitute parties after action has started;
- on its own initiative or on application
- But permission of Court always required to add or substitute parties once claim form served.

2 types of Additional claims;
3rd-party claims - can only be made D
- D can make linked claims against person not yet party to action; a 3rd party claim;
- CPR includes these as **additional claims**, with <u>counterclaims</u> and <u>claims between existing Ds</u>
- When bringing in a 3rd-party, **Part 20 claim form** must be issued and served on all Ps including one added
- If third-party claim issued before or at same time as defence filed, no permission of Court needed;
- otherwise permission is required
[It is because the defence and 3rd-party claim interact that filing of defence is point at which permission needed. If defence already

served, the defence document will need to be recalled, amended and re-served]
- D can initiate a claim against third-party via:
- Contribution claim;
- Claim that 3rd party is wholly or partly to blame for the C's loss

- Indemnity claim
- Claim that 3rd party is under obligation to D (usually via contract) to reimburse some or all of what D ordered to pay:
- e.g.: insurance
- "Any other remedy"
- CPR gives D free reign to claim any other remedy from a third-party;
- for Court in exercise of discretion and case management to detach claims it feels should not be heard together
Much of additional claim procedure mimics that for main action including;
- response pack must accompany Part 20 claim form;
- third party's failure to respond can result in default judgement etc.;
- see chapter 8.

Additional claims against co-defendants (party-to-party claims)
- Where 2 Ds are already Ps to action they can make same sorts of claims against one another, as above
- if co-D wants judge to use existing powers to apportion liability, no formal notice needed; saves expense;
- if some other issue or claim made between co-Ds:
  - order for disclosure of documents; or
  - claim for an indemnity, for example;
- **Part 20 claim** form must be issued and served (see chapter 8)

***

CHAPTER 6

Statements of case (SoC) – also see Chapter 4 for more detail

- Claim form is the lead document of a generic collection of documents called "Statements of Case" which include:
  - claim form;
  - particulars of claim;
  - acknowledgements of service;
  - defence;
  - reply;
- Part 7 claim is concise statement in **claim form** and particulars of claim of:
  - nature of claim;
  - remedy sought;
  - redress.
- Claim form must state PoC attached or will follow.
- If C making **claim to money** must state:
  - amounts claimed;
  - amount for allocation where C cannot say how much expects to recover (< £10 K, £10k-£25k, >£25k+);
  - if claim for PI, C must state whether value of claim < £1k or > £1k;
- if claim specifies exact sum of money must include:
  - rate of interest claimed;
  - date from which interest claimed;
  - date to which calculated;
  - total amount of interest claimed;
  - daily rate at which accruing.
- **Particulars of Claim** must include PABLIR (Parties, Agreement, Breach Loss, Interest, Remedy) and:
  - concise statement of facts;
  - whether C seeks interest and whether interest under contract or by act of Parliament;

- grounds for any aggravated or exemplary damages;
- grounds for any provisional damages claimed.
- **Statement of truth** required in every statement of case:
  - if not given, P may not rely on statement as evidence of matters set out;
  - Court may strike out statement of case;
  - innocent party can also apply to strike out C's case.
- **If claim in HC, C must state:**
  - value of claim > £100k
  - value of claim >or= £ 50k, in PI claims, and
  - which list C would like case to be in.
- **If claim for PI, C must give:**
  - DOB;
  - details of injuries;
  - schedule of past and future losses;
  - medical report if relying on one;
  - details if C's condition may worsen;
- P may refer to any point of law on which relying and serve any doc feels necessary.

Step	Time
C **issues claim form** with court	C has **4 months to serve** claim form
Court **serves claim form on D**	C has **14 days to serve particulars of claim** on D
C **serves particulars of claim** on D	Important; D has only 14 **days** to file: acknowledgement of service; or defense (must be served on every other party)
If D files : **acknowledgement of service**	D then has **28 days** from receipt of particular claim to file defence and C and D may agree to extend time for defence for up to 28 days

If D fails to file AoS or defense within 14 days (or the 28 after AoS)	C may obtain default judgement.
D files defence	D may make a counterclaim in defence doc
Court sends Ps notice of **provisional allocation**	Depending on track Ps have; **14** or **28** days to complete **directions questionnaire [DQ]**– see chapt 12 14 days – small claims track; 28 Days – other tracks;
C may file reply to D's defense and if needed, defense to counterclaim	Reply optional but must be filed with DQ.
Either P	may make application for further info
If D fails to file AoS or defense	If **6 months** passes without C entering or applying for default or summary judgement, claim stayed. Either P may apply to lift stay.

Acknowledgement of Service, Defences, Replies and Counterclaims:
Time periods: CPR 15 and 16

- Court has discretion to order claim will continue without AoS or defense **or any other statement of case.**

Defence must state:
- which allegation in PoC **denied** and reasons for denial;
- if different version of events relied on, details must be given of version;
- which allegations D **unable to admit or deny** and requires C to prove;
- which allegations D **admits**;

- if D disputes C's statement of value must say why and give estimate to value;
- if D has not filed AoS, must give address for service in defence.
- **defence of set off:** if D contends he is owed money by C and relies on that as defense to all or part of C's claim;
- D may include details in defence and claim C's liability should be **set off** against own.
- where C has only claimed money; and D states in defense notice the money has been paid to C:
  - Court will **send claimant's notice** to C asking if C wishes proceedings to continue;
  - if he does, C must serve copy on D;
  - if C fails to respond, claim stayed.

Reply, optional:
- If C wishes to reply; should file **reply with directions questionnaire;**
- after reply, permission required for subsequent statements of case.

Effect of not responding to allegations:
Responding in a defence:
- D who fails to respond to allegation in defence statement is taken to admit allegation;
- if D sets out nature of his defense, D taken as requiring proof of allegation;
- in money claim unless D expressly admits amount, D taken as requiring proof of amount.
Responding in reply:
- replies optional – failure to reply does not lead to admissions;
- failure to reply taken as requiring proof

- where **six months** after period for filing a defense
  - D has not served or filed admission, defense or counterclaim and
  - C has not sought default judgement or summary judgement
  - **claim automatically stayed.**

- Any P can apply to have it lifted.

Summary;

- D must respond to allegations in their defence doc to avoid making admissions or concessions;
- replies are optional;
- time periods in table strictly adhered to by Court.

***

Sett's aside judgment entered after Striking out –

A party can apply to court to have judgment against them (after struck out) set aside.

An application must be made not more than 14 days after judgment been served

CHAPTER 7

Remedies. Claiming Damages; Contract and Tort

Contract:
- if contract breached, damages available as of right;
- C required to take reasonable steps to reduce loss and avoid action that may increase loss;
- damages assessed at time of breach;
- calculated at either expectation interest or reliance interest;
- **Expectation interest** is normal, damages look **forward;**
  - puts C in position he would have been in **had contract been performed,** includes both:
  - loss of promise of performance; and
  - loss of profit resulting;
    - o   In either case, loss cannot be too remote
- **Reliance interest:** amount C lost in reliance on contract;
  - used when C cannot show what he would have lost but can show what he has lost;
  - cannot use reliance interest if contract would have been bad bargain.

Remoteness - Limitation on compensation:
- Hadley v Baxendale; loss must be in reasonable contemplation of both Ps;
  - must flow naturally from breach; or
  - loss contemplated as a **serious possibility** by both parties.
- Addis v Gramophone: general rule **damages for distress/ disappointment** not available following breach-of-contract;
- Farley v Skinner: where purpose of contract is C's enjoyment or to prevent C's distress; example is a holiday,
  - damages can be sought for breach (pleasure and enjoyment);
  - award usually limited £10,000.

Tort:
- equitable remedies are at discretion of courts;
- damages aim to putting victim back in position would have been in **had tort not been committed;**
- C required to take reasonable steps to reduce loss and avoid action that may increase loss;
- aim is to compensate victims for loss.

Reduction of damages:
- some losses maybe too **remote** to be recoverable (Wagonmound);
- damages in tort may also be reduced by contributory negligence; or D's failure to mitigate.

3 categories Aggravated damages may be awarded in Tort:
- compensatory and awarded when C's conduct especially reprehensible and causes C special loss;
  - oppressive, arbitrary or unconstitutional actions by government servants;
  - when D's conduct calculated to make profit beyond C's compensation;
  - if expressly authorised by statute.

Provisional damages; s32 Senior Courts Act 1981 possible
- if a chance is proved or admitted that C will suffer serious deterioration or develop serious disease in future;
- C given initial award [general damages] with possibility to make future claim if tort occurs.

Contract
Specific performance:
- order of court requiring a P to complete a performance of contractual obligations;
- before court will order specific performance C must show:
  - damages would be inadequate remedy;
  - **Uniqueness** of thing contracted for ; and
  - ineffectiveness of damages to compensate C; e.g. sale of Ming vase
- Specific performance unlikely to be granted for contracts requiring:
  - Supervision;
  - building contracts;

- contracts for personal services
- Will be refused if order would cause severe hardship to D

Injunctions: see chapter 18.

- mandatory injunction; must do an act;
- prohibitory injunctions; D must not do an act;
- mandatory orders, harder to obtain.
- Injunction can either be final or interim;
- Injunction to breach-of-contract may be ordered in support of Cs contractual rights or following an actual or threatened breach by D;
- Where breach merely threatened, higher degree of proof required

Rescission:

- rescinded contract is set aside;
- Ps restored to position would have been in had contract never been made;
- for contract, recession available in 3 situations only:
  - misrepresentation; [M]
  - undue influence ; [U]
  - duress. [D]

- **4 equitable limits to rescission:**
  - Restitutio in integrum; impossible to return parties to position prior to contract - product used;
  - 3rd party acquired rights for value without notice re contract [protected as equity's darling];
  - C affirmed contract;
  - unreasonable delay by C between discovering serious breach and seeking to rescind.

- **Rectification** - terms of contract may be incorrectly set down :
  - court may order correction of contract to reflect true agreement;
  - possible remedy where mistake by both parties in recording contract.

Damages in lieu of rescission

- **S 2 (2) misrepresentation act 1967** Court has power to award damages in lieu of rescission;
- damages should not exceed expectation interest.

Claiming interest on money remedies in tort:

- Court has discretion to award interest on any part of damages awarded;
- from date of cause of action until date of payment or judgement;
- Interest on judgement debts distinct from interest on damages;
- Interest on damages compensates for loss of use of money C would otherwise have had
- Interest on judgement debts to encourage payment of debts
- General rule; interest runs from date of judgement CPR 40.8
- If contract between C and D fixes interest rate on judgement debts, Court has no power to fix different rate
- If no such contract agreement exists court can charge **Debt interest** as follows

Statute	Interest rate	Application
County Court Interest of Judgement Debts Order 1991	8%	All CC judgements over £5000
Judgement Act 1838	8%	All HC judgements
Late Payment of Commercial Debts Interest Act 1998	8% above official dealing rate	contract for supply goods or services where purchaser and supplier **each acting in the course of a business**

***

CHAPTER 8

Multiple Causes of Action, Counterclaims & Part 20 etc.

Multiple Ps [CPR 19.3]
- where multiple Ps hold same right, all must be joined as Cs;
- if do not consent, should add as Ds;
- where liability joined but not several, every person jointly liable must be made D

Addition of new P [CPR 19.2] and substitution – see chapter 9

NB;
- if ONLY correcting spelling of name use CPR 17.4 (amendment to statement of case after expiry of limitation period)
  If you get a mistake question use;
- S 35 Limitation Act test
- CPR 17.4
- CPR 19.5.

***

CHAPTER 9

Amendment of Statement of Case CPR17.1

- After filing or service, a party may wish to amend their statement of case*;
- *Generic name for typical documents setting out the party's case including:*
  - *claim form;*
  - *particulars of claim;*
  - *defense;*
  - *reply;*
  - *additional claim forms etc.*
  - Amendment often happens after disclosure of documents, when other evidential information comes to light.
  - Generally, overriding objective of dealing with cases justly means, if made in time, <u>amendments are uncontroversial;</u>
  - it is important the real issues are litigated;
  - problems can arise if a P seeks to amend late or after limitation period expired.

Amendments to Statement of Case before expiry of relevant limitation period.
Before service:
1. P can amend statement of case at any time before it served on other P; no permission of court required;
2. application to disallow such amendments should be made within **14 days of service**;
3. Court may disallow but if other P has not yet seen it, usually no big deal to change document before they do.
4. **Power of court to disallow amendments CPR 17.2:**
   - Even if C amended statement of case where permission of court not required;
   - Court may still disallow amendment;

- to challenge amendments opposing party, must apply within **14 days of service** of amended statement of case.

After service, within limitation period:
- After statement of case served, can only amend, either with:
  - written consent of Ps; or
  - permission of court; unless
- amendment involves a change of party, when permission of Court always required.
  [This is sensible; the court is happy for parties to sort out nature of allegations between themselves. If different Ps are to become involved, Court would like to know.]
  - Main consideration when adding, substituting or removing a P is whether amendment desirable to ensure all relevant issues in dispute can be resolved.
  - This is matter for Court decide

Determining an application for permission to amend- PD 17:
- No specific guidance re how court exercises its discretion;
- Court guided by overriding objective;
- In accordance with overriding objective, Court decides where justice lies:
  - provided amendment required to determine all relevant issues, justice almost always lies with P seeking to amend;
  - unless other P can show they will be prejudiced (above time and cost of redrafting statements in response etc., which can usually be dealt with by costs order).
- Dramatic **Cobbold v Greenwich**; amendments should in general be allowed
- Permission to amend defence will be denied if no real prospect of success.
- **Mills and Reeve**; authority puts;
- heavy burden on P making late amendment to demonstrate will not put Ps on unequal footing; or
- jeopardise other P's preparation for trial

- Where is so prejudiced, an amendment may be allowed even after hearing of evidence at trial
- A P will not be prejudiced where had opportunity to make submissions on new case and would not have called new evidence in response to it.

Costs of amending:

- usual order: P making amendment pays costs <u>of and arising from</u> amendment;
- if a P unreasonably fails to consent to amendment, forcing unnecessary application to court, may be ordered:
  - amending P pays costs occasioned by amendment (as these arise anyway) and;
  - unreasonable P pays costs of avoidable application to Court

Seeking permission

- Permission to amend sought by application notice [PD17], applicant should file:
  - application notice; and
  - copy of statement of case with proposed amendments;
  - application will be dealt with at hearing;
  - may be dealt with on papers if P's consent or Court considers it unnecessary to hold hearing;
  - if new P to be added or substituted, written evidence should set out new P's connection with claim;
  - Otherwise, evidence may not be necessary if purpose of change clear from amended statement of case which must be filed with application
- In practice the original and amended statement of case are submitted to help court know what is proposed
- Applications normally dealt with as part of court's case management function by Master or district judge
- If necessary, application may be made to trial judge.

Amendment to Statement of Case after of relevant limitation period.

- General rule: P may not amend once relevant limitation period has expired as;
- costs can not compensate for injustice caused by proposed amendment after limitation period has expired;

  [if amendment would deprive P of defence that the action is statute barred, it is not normally allowed]

  Three types of exceptions

1. **Amendments having effect of adding a new claim** which Court **may** allow, if satisfied change in keeping with overriding objective:

- adding or substituting a claim if it arises out of substantially the same facts already in issue;
- adding or substituting a new PI claim where limitation period disapplied under s 33 (see chapter 2);
- allowing P to raise counterclaim or setoff <u>for the first time</u>:
  - counterclaims and setoffs deemed to commence on same date as original claim,

2. **Amendments having effect of adding a new P, may** be allowed where:

  [Note pure additions are not allowed; only substitutions.]

- Court exercised discretion under s 33 to disapply limitation period in PI action

  [This discretion can result in a new P in same way as a new claim, or both together]

- amendment only alters legal capacity in which a P claims, provided capacity is one P had when proceedings started or has since acquired
- amendment is necessary which is only possible where;
  - original P died or been declared bankrupt and his interest or liability has passed to a new P
  - amendment legally necessary to maintain the action
  - has been a mistake naming a party to original action:
    - Court must be satisfied person who made mistake was person responsible for issuing claim form, or his agent;

- applicant must show had mistake not been made, new P would have been named in claim form;
- mistake has to be of the name, not the identity of the P (Sardinia Sulcis test).
- no injustice should be caused if application is granted. (e.g.; if P to be substituted would be taken by surprise by amendment Court may exercise its discretion to refuse to allow)

3. **Amendments having effect of adding a new defence**
- General rule: court will allow D to amend the defence after limitation has expired unless C can show effect of amendment is to blame another P whom the C cannot now sue and
- D is at fault in not seeking to amend earlier

Note:
- Court will not grant D permission to amend statement of case where effect would transfer responsibility for claim to new P who cannot be sued by C because C time-barred.
- If facts indicate new P could have been sued prior to commencing proceedings, D may be allowed to amend since C effectively elected not to pursue proposed new P.

Cost consequences of amending:
- General rule: where amendment allowed P seeking to amend must pay other side's consequential costs including:
- application / preparation for application / knock on amendments e.g. to other statements of case
- Cost considerations must be central when thinking about making application to amend.
- If C seeks reasonable amendments to statement of case early, D should consider consenting as unreasonable refusal to consent may result in loss of usual costs order
- P should seek consent of other Ps before seeking permission of Court as may save cost of application
- CPR 17 and PD 17 provide definitive guidance re how court should exercise discretion re application to amend

Counterclaims and contribution notices - Part 20:
- additional claim is claim brought by P other than C, following C's claim:
- **Type one**; counterclaim by D against C, or another person;
- **Type two**; additional claim by D against another person, who may be a current P;
- **Type three**; additional claim by new P [6]
- With exception of counterclaims, all additional claims brought using Part 20 and treated as claim for purposes of CPR

Part 20 claim must include:
- main claim number;
- details of C and D;
- brief details of additional claim;
- statement of value;
- name and address of third-party;
- particulars of claim;
- statement of truth;

- CPR 10 - rules re acknowledgement of service do **not apply** to C defending counterclaim
- CPR 12 - default judgement rules do **not apply** to additional claims by D or new party claiming additionally.

Effect on additional claims if main proceedings determined without trial:
- additional claim is treated as separate claim;
- determination of main claim by settlement/ strikeout will not always determine additional claim;
- whether any point continuing with additional claim depends on relief sought;
- where D claims indemnity or contribution from 3rd party and main claim is dismissed or stuck out, there will be no need for the additional claim.
Summary;

---

[6] CPR 27

- Different rules apply depending on who brings additional claim and who against;
- purpose of part 20; enable additional claims to be managed in cost-effective way avoiding diverging judgements.

***

CHAPTER 10

Request Further Information [Info] CPR 18.1

Requests for further info under Part 18:
- used to seek clarification or get info about matter in dispute, whether or not referred to in statement of case;
- useful litigation tool to test weakness in opponent's case, enables requesting P to "know" case to be met;
- Part 18 request does not apply to small claims track, although court may order P to clarify case

Requests should be made:
- as soon as practicable after need arises;
- before making application for CPR 18.1 order, should make preliminary request first;
- preliminary request must be restricted to what necessary and proportionate;
- P seeking further info should serve written request on other P, leaving appropriate time for response;
- if possible by email.

Requests only granted where they are:
- reasonably necessary;
- proportionate;
- Application determined by reference to proportionality and in accordance with overriding objective;
- Following application for order under Part 18, court has discretion to make order having regard to:
  - likely benefit;
  - likely cost of giving it;
  - whether financial resources of P2 sufficient to enable compliance.
- Court can use procedure on own initiative to order P to clarify or give additional info;
- P2 must file response and serve on all Ps.

Response to request for further info; PD 18 (2.1-2.4) must be:
- Within the time specified (by court if appropriate);
- in writing;
- dated;
- signed by respondent party or representative;
- verified by statement of truth;
- where request by letter, responding P may respond by letter or formal reply;
- if letter; must clearly identify as response to request and must not contain any unrelated matter;
- unless P2 responds on same doc, PD 18 requires response to mirror elements of request;
- when responding P2 serves copy on every other P, must copy the request and response on the courts;
- only in absence of proper response should application be made to court.
- **response becomes statement of case.**

Summary:
- Before making application for CPR 18.1 order, P should make preliminary request first;
- Court may order further info on own initiative;
- usual way to set out response is in question/ answer format.

***

CHAPTER 11

Default Judgement and Summary Judgement.

Default Jugement [DJ] CPR Part 12 :
- with limited exceptions (consumer credit and Part 8 claims), C may obtain DJ in any claim;
- particulars of claim when served must be accompanied by a response pack; forms give D range of options for responding including:
  - acknowledgement of service;
  - admissions and defence;
  - counterclaim.
- Once particulars of claim served, D wanting to defend must:
  - acknowledge service within 14 days and file defence within 28 days, of service of particulars of claim; or
  - skip acknowledgement and file defense within 14 days, of service of service of particulars of claim
  [filing acknowledgement of service buys D time].
- Ps can agree to extend time for filing defence for up to further 28 days, D should notify Court if agreed
  Default judgement possible in 2 situations:
  - D failed to file either acknowledgement of service or defence in time; or
  - having filed acknowledgement of service, D failed to file defence in time
  [Default judgement also possible where D files counterclaim and C fails to file defence to counterclaim within relevant time period].
  How default judgement obtained:
- money claim (including claims re delivery of goods where C will accept money instead); default judgement is an administrative process, available by filing request form at Court office by filling;
- permission by application notice to Court is necessary where:

- non money claims; such as equitable relief; and
- in money claims with exceptional features including where C claiming:
  - o only costs;
  - o against child or protected party [litigation friend must be appointed before DJ entered]
  - o in tort against civil partner

Application Notice per Parts 23 procedure for interim applications:
- in writing;
- usually on notice;
- supported by evidence about nature of claim and
- written evidence to show meets procedural requirements below;
- provide D's date of birth
- there will be hearing
- Court will give judgement it appears C entitled to on his statement of case.

Procedural prerequisites:
- Court satisfied D served with particulars of claim;
  [if Court did not serve, C must prove by certificate of service]
  - time limit for filing acknowledgement of service or defence must have expired;
  - D must not have either:
  - admitted claim and asked for time to pay;
  - satisfied claim;
  - applied for summary judgement; or   }
  - applied to have C's case struck out   } *and these application have not been disposed of*

Types of judgements in money claims:
- If claim for specified amount of money plus interest; judgement will be final re liability and amount (inc interest)
- Where claim for unspecified amount of money or damages or asks Court to decide quantum of interest, judgement will be partial or interlocutory:

- final re D's liability to pay damages; but
- amount to be paid to be determined; date of future hearing to decide will be fixed.

Setting aside default judgement:
- D who has default DJ entered against him can apply to have it:
  - varied; or
  - set aside;
- application made using Part 23 Procedure for interim applications.
- default judgement **must** be set aside as of right if wrongly entered i.e. procedural requirements of part 12 not met such as time for acknowledging service has not expired;
- otherwise default judgement **may** be set aside or varied if appears to Court looking at evidence that:
  - D has **real prospect of successfully** defending claim; or
  - **some other good reason** to set aside, vary judgement or let D defend claim.
- Court must take into account whether application to set aside made promptly;
- Any claim abandoned by C to secure a default judgement will be restored if judgement set aside

Real Prospect of success:
- wording invokes summary judgement test (chapter 12);
- real prospect means **better than merely arguable** (ED&F v Patel); does not require case will probably succeed;
- burden of proof on applicant;
- court should focus not on initial procedural failure but on and doing justice;
- recent cases highlight importance of promptness in applications; even where defense might succeed at trial delay of more than 60 days unlikely to be prompt.

Summary Judgment: Tm to serve eviden
on parties 14 days befor th hear'g
Applicat'n must be supported by evidence,

Civil Litigation

D to serve evidue on C - 7 das
befor heaus,
            C - to serve furthr eviels
                                3 days
                                befor
                              heeny

Some other good reason:

- due to deeming provisions, D may be considered properly served though particulars of claim never arrived
- not a procedural defect but could amount to a good reason to set aside despite there not otherwise being a real prospect of success;
- e.g. D may have paid up rather than have embarrassing judgement entered against him;
- unconscionable behaviour on part of C may also amount to good reason.

- Where Court sets aside default judgement it may impose conditions:
- most common condition; D pay costs thrown away incurred as a result of any failure to follow rules;
- D may be ordered to pay whole or part of disputed sum in to court *[must not be for amount D cannot possibly meet as would be roundabout way of giving judgement to C].*

Summary judgement [SJ] CPR Part 24

- aim: to provide early judgement in cases where D has no realistic hope of success;
- with few exceptions (residential repossession) summary judgement may be given in any type of case.
- In **Striking out:** D must set out clearly where issue taken with claim. Incoherent or meaningless defenses are liable to be struck out – see chapter 12
- **Summary judgement is overlapping procedure use where:** whatever D says, however clearly;
  - incapable of succeeding as a defense and
  - no other compelling reason why case should continue to trial

Claimant's application for Summary Judgement

- Application should be made as soon as possible.
- Unless court gives permission;
- C may only apply for SJ:
  - after D has responded to particulars of claim by

- filing an acknowledgement of service or
- defence (failure to respond to claim would mean C could seek default judgement, above)
- and before filing applicant's directions questionnaire (*which asks first if summary judgement application pending*).

Application is made as Interim Applications under CPR 23:
- in writing;
- notice must be given to respondent at least **14 days** before hearing (rather than usual 3);
- must contain evidence in support of any point of law or provision and
- statement of belief that there is:
  - no defence with a real prospect of success or
  - other reason for trial of the action;
- defendant's evidence in reply must be filed at least **7 days** before hearing;
- if applicant wishes to respond, further evidence must be filed at least **3 days** before hearing.
- Once application by C made, D may need not file a defence before hearing.
- Applications heard by district judge in CC or master in HC.
- At **hearing** court must consider D has
  - no real prospect of success; and
  - no other compelling reason to have a trial

No real prospect of success
- It is a serious matter to deprive D of right to put defence at trial so standard of proof high.
- In Swain v Hillman, Lord Wolf said words "no real prospect of success" are self-explanatory:
  Real means realistic not fanciful; possible not necessarily probable

- He emphasised summary judgement not meant to dispense with trial where are issues which should be considered and tested.

- If D's case has some prospects of success, summary judgement should be refused.
- Nor are summary judgement applications mini trials, rather hearings to determine to what extent ought to be a trial.

No compelling reason for a trial
- Sometimes Court may feel D has little or no prospect of success but there is some other compelling reason for trial; for example:
    - in a complex case; or
    - if C's actions appear discreditable;
  In case of Miles v Bull:
- farmer sold farmhouse to C whilst his wife still living in it;
- wife had not registered her rights of occupation;
- she was not protected against new owner;
- wife did not have defence in law;
- new owner sued wife for possession and applied for summary judgement.
  Court held: husband and new owner had conducted business in underhand way;
- wife ought to have access to litigation process to test owners claim;
- owner ought to be put to strict proof of claim for justice to be done.

Burden of proof:
- CPR 24.2 is not explicit re where burden of proof lies;
- Court interprets rule as placing burden on applicant to show D's case not worthy of trial;
- when D applies to set aside default judgement, burden on D to show his case has real prospect of success;
- Judge will not weigh up merits of case except to determine whether some point in having a trial;
- every case is looked at individually.
- Court is not liable to take every assertion at face value and will reject;
    - incorrect legal argument; or
    - evidence which is implausible or irrelevant.

- The case of P opposing summary judgement must appear to have some credibility of that P's allegations.

Possible orders on claimant's application:
- **Judgement for C:**
- C normally gets order for costs of application.
- **Conditional order:**
- if appears to Court it is possible a defence will succeed but improbable if may be willing to let defence continue on strict conditions for example;
- D pays some money in to court failing which C gets judgement:
  - Court must not impose condition unless some prospect D can comply (*as tantamount to C getting judgement*);
  - onus on D to establish inability to meet condition.
- Requiring D to take particular step in litigation such as filing more detailed defence, may also be a condition
- Normal costs order; cost in the case.
- If application dismissed; where D has chance of success or some other compelling reason to have a trial, costs of interim application normally go to D.

Expansion of summary judgement to D
- D may apply for summary judgement to attack hopelessly weak claim;
- summary judgement for D will be granted when Court considers C has:
  - no real prospect of success and
  - no other compelling reason to have a trial
- Same principles, procedure and range of orders above apply to D's application;
- Ds application for summary judgement is also possible in any sort of case.
  [Another possible order by Court in summary judgement proceedings is striking out or dismissal of whole or some issues in C's action]

Court's initiative
- Court can fix summary judgement hearing on own initiative: if senses weak claim or defence.
- Procedure also used to obtain summary determination of issues where court satisfied they do not require full investigation, to reduce complexity and length of trial.

Counterclaims, Set Off and Summary Judgement.
- When D make claims against C, included in same proceedings as C's action, known as counterclaim
- **Set-off is a special kind of counterclaim;** special ability to operate as a defence (to extent of set off);
- highly relevant to outcome of summary judgements.
- Example;
- C claims £6000
- D pleads nothing except set off of £4000; defence of £4000 but no other answer to claim.
- Summary judgement or order will be: for the C £2000
- Dismissal of C's action re the £4000;
- Leaves D free to continue defence or seek summary judgement himself re £4000

Three sets off situations:
Mutual debts
- D owes C £5000, C owes D £3000, if C sues for £5000, D can set off £3000
- The amounts need not be debts so long as *ascertained amounts are owed*

Supply Contract setoff
- Applies where goods or services supplied under contract re which C sues, claimed by D to be defective
- Where C sues for price of goods or services, D can set off any claim for defects in quality of same goods or services

Equitable setoff

- D's counterclaim can be treated as equitable setoff, even if not technically setoff in law.
- Where counterclaim and C's claim arise out of same contract, or transaction so inextricably linked that would be unfair to uphold one without other, equity intervenes to treat cross claim as a set off.
- Classic example; landlord and tenant cases: typically tenant sued by landlord for rent arrears.
- Tenant can set off a counterclaim for damages for breach of same tenancy agreement; such as failure to repair

Not all counterclaims are set offs
- Where counterclaim is not a setoff it has no defensive capacity (cannot stop C getting summary judgement)
- May be appropriate to delay or stay execution of SJ until determination of counterclaim where there is:
  - sufficient connection between claim and counterclaim;
  - unresolved issue between Ps and / or;
  - some other compelling reason
- In determining whether counterclaim justifies stay of execution, Court will consider:
  - connection between claim and counterclaim (closer the connection, stronger the case to stay)
  - strength of counterclaim (stronger the counterclaim, better case will be) and
  - ability of C to satisfy judgement D might obtain on counterclaim (doubt strengthens case for stay.)
- Predicting when a stay of execution will be granted is tricky;
- in Peter Robinson Limited, Court of Appeal considered lack of clarity a good thing because gives Courts useful room to manoeuvre in individual cases.

The cheque rule; defensive capabilities of set off
- There is no defence to a bad cheque;
- when you pay by cheque promise to pay is as good as cash;
- rule applies to any form of promissory note, including direct debits;

- legally operation of rule explained by existence two separate agreements.
- There is no defence to a bad cheque, only exception is if cheque was obtained:
  - by fraud;
  - misrepresentation; or
  - contract void; if underlying contract nullified so no money should have changed hands.
- Very limited exceptions highlighted by Sachs LJ;
  The court will "not whittle away this rule of practice by introducing unnecessary exceptions under influence of sympathy invoking stories."

Timeline for summary judgement application:

Step A	Comment
D files AoS or defence	C cannot apply until D has filed either; AoS or Defence
C/A makes application	D/R must have **14 days'** notice of hearing date and issues to be decided
D/R files and serve evidence	D/R must file and serve evidence no less than **7 days** before hearing
C/A files and serve evidence in reply	A must file and serve evidence in reply no less than **3 days** before hearing

Chapter summary:
- summary judgement and default judgements entirely different;
- default judgement sought where D failed to file and serve a defence;
- summary judgement is where either party considers there should be no trial at all

***

CHAPTER 12

Case Management, Track Allocation, Sanctions and Striking out.

Case allocation - only applies where liability contested:

- After defence filed court official provisionally allocates case to track, largely based on value;
- notice of proposed allocation served on each P requires each P to file completed directions questionnaire [DQ] and serve on each other:
  - in small claims; no less than **14 days** after notice of proposed allocation; and
  - other tracks; no less than **28 days.**
- If P unrepresented, Court sends DQ otherwise notice informs Ps how to obtain one; internet etc.
- notice may require parties to file:
  - proposed directions, by same date, if case looks suitable for fast or multitrack; or
  - cost budgets or disclosure reports, in multitrack;
- if P fails to complete DQ in time in CC money claim, reminder sent then claim or defence struck out;
- in other cases, Court makes order it sees fit, may include striking out.
- Typically, defaulter meets cost.
- Once completed DQ filed, procedural judge, Master or District Judge, makes official allocation:
- if Ps in Court before this, allocation may be dealt with then; to use time efficiently;
- allocation will be deferred where stay requested / ordered, to allow for early settlement;
- Court may not hold allocation hearing and Ps may be notified in writing by notice of allocation;

- track to which case allocated should reflect:
  - **value**, excluding: costs, interest and amounts not in dispute
  - **case management needs**; legal or factual complexity, remedy sought, importance of outcome to wider persons, extent of oral evidence required, etc.
- Court entitled to allocate claim to higher or lower track then financial value indicates;
- overriding objective requires cases dealt with fairly and cost effectively and track options helps with this.
- Court has power to subsequently reallocate case to different track [CPR 26.10]

CPR 29.4 - Ps required to endeavor to agree directions in all cases:

- Where P unable to agree; counsel make submissions on directions, before court makes order;
- court has specific powers conferred under other rules and may make order on own initiative without need for application;
- where court proposes order of own initiative it;
  - may give affected P opportunity to make representations;
  - if does, must specify time and manner of representations.
- **Court may make order of own initiative** without hearing and without representation by either P.
- Court's order must state an affected P has right to apply to Court to have order set aside/ varied / stayed ; and
- if court does not specify time for such application, P has **7 days to apply**.

Small Claims Track:

- normal track for defended claims not exceeding £10,000;
- some exceptions only referred to fast track:
  - allegations of dishonesty;
  - landlord and tenant cases;
  - PI claims where value of PSLA exceeds >£1000.

Features of small claims track include:
- **Allocation,** fixes date for hearing and length;
- standard directions given including:
  - exchanging only documents each party will rely on;
  - bringing original documents to hearing;
  - obligation to inform Court if case settles.
- **Many usual features of litigation are missing including:**
- order for disclosure;
- most interim remedies, except injunction;
- most case management directions;
- most evidential rules;
- part 36 offers;
- traditional approach to conducting proceedings missing:
  - evidence not usually given on oath;
  - hearing conducted informally by District Judge;
  - no expert evidence without Court permission.
- **Track designed for layperson:**
  - scope to recover costs limited to disbursements and out-of-pocket expenses;
  - restriction applies to original hearing and subsequent appeal.

Fast-track includes:
- most defended claims falling within £10,001 - £25,000;
- cases taking no more than a day.
- **Hallmarks of FastTrack include:**
- few interim hearings;
- standard directions, Court may make standard directions form bespoke as necessary;
- trial date fixed by court when case allocated;
- limited experts: single joint expert evidence by written report;
- one-day trial, if runs over judge will normally sit next day;
- trial judge may depart from procedural judge's directions;
- most witness statement stand as evidence in chief;
- trial costs fixed with summary assessment of costs;
- cases actively managed to tight timetable no longer than **30 weeks;**

- case management directions given at only 2 stages, if possible without hearing, at:
- track allocation; and
- filing pre-trial checklists [PTC]

Directions at allocation typically lay down case management timetable for:

- trial date / window;
- identification of and exchange of evidence; witness statements, expert evidence etc.;
- physical hearing only held if necessary.

Pre-trial directions:

- standard form directions are tailored to individual case. Focus on:
- checking compliance with previous directions;
- how evidence to be received;
- agreeing and filing bundles;
- time allocated for examination / cross-examination; advocates may need to be focused in questioning;
- Ps should seek to agree directions which Court can endorse, if sees fit;
- C must pay <u>hearing fee,</u> refundable if case settles before trial
* if fee unpaid reminder issued and if unpaid claim struck out.
- Not less than **2 days** before trial both parties file statement of costs;
- compliance with timetable encouraged; minor variations can be agreed by Ps in writing without court approval up to 28 days but **3 dates must not be adversely affected:**
    1. returning directions questionnaire [DQ];
    2. returning pre-trial checklists [PTC];
    3. trial date;
- these dates only change with Court permission, trial date only changed in exceptional circumstances.
- Costs normally summarily assessed at end of trial fixed by reference to value of claim.

Multitrack for cases where:

- more than £25,000 claimed;
- closer management required;

- more than one-day trial required;
- Part 8 claims and specialist proceedings are usually multitrack;
- multitrack cases often expensive and CPR focuses on ensuring cost managed;
- if direction or order applied for not considered proportionate or relevant, it should not be given.

As with other tracks, once case allocated to multitrack court will give directions:

- directions will be case-sensitive;
- docketing means case allocated to specific procedural judge responsible for all management & giving directions;
- parties encouraged to agree directions, submitting to Court for approval to reduce cost;
  - is ultimately for Court to decide directions.
- When giving case management direction, Ps and Court should use standard directions template.
- Much case management done on papers, where that not possible one of following may be necessary:

Case management conferences [CMC]:

- used by Court to manage case progress, focus on timetable to trial;
- can be held immediately on allocation;
- purpose to ensure:
  - real issues identified;
  - directions given;
  - case managed according to needs;
- notice given to both Ps at least **3 clear days** before first CMC and Ps must file and serve in non-PI cases:
  - disclosure reports;
  - proposed directions; and
  - if possible, agreed cost budgets.

Court will:

- review statements of case and allocate case to track, if has not happened already;
- check compliance with previous orders or directions;
- review cost budgets and revise if necessary;

- record agreements on conduct of case;
- make directions needed;
- promote use of ADR with stay if appropriate;
- typical directions will set times for; **DEExT:**
  - disclosure;
  - exchange of WS;
  - expert reports;
  - filing of pre-trial checklists;
  - trial date;
  - amendment to statement of case;
  - use of witness summaries;
  - if something arises not necessarily dealt with as part of case management, such as application for interim payments likely to be opposed, C should issue in time for hearing CMC

Cost management regime [CMR]:
- involves courts managing steps and costs in litigation to further the overriding objective.
- All Part 7 multitrack cases are governed by **CMR** unless:
- worth in excess of >£10 million; or
- case subject of fixed cost;
- Court has discretion to apply CMR to any case or disapply it;
- CMR sets overall budget proportionate to case;
- case management decisions are based on that budget;
- before making any case management decision, Court will have regard to: **CPR 3.7:**
  - budgets of Ps; and
  - cost of procedural steps;
- projected costs budgets are prepared by Ps and, if agreed, approved by Court;
- set out how much each P expects each litigation stage to cost;
- each P must file and exchange cost budget, verified by statement of truth, by dates directed;
- if no date directed, must be **7 days before first CMC**;

- if Ps exchange but cannot agree budgets Court fixes recoverable amount using cost management order **[CMO]**;
- Court will make CMO unless satisfied litigation can be conducted justly, at proportionate cost, without it;
- **In CMO court will record;**
  1. parts of budget agreed by Ps
  2. where parts not agreed; Court makes its own revisions, then records its approval;
  3. (once Ps have agreed parts of budget, Court cannot alter them, such agreement minimizes risk);
  4. it can refuse to make CMO if regards those parts as disproportionate or unreasonable
- Court may convene **cost management conference;** to address costs management;
- CPR encourages courts to conduct cost management conference; by telephone or in writing where possible;
- failure to file cost budget, treated as filing budget containing relevant Court fees; **CPR3.14:** unless Court orders otherwise,
- Ps are required to give an estimate of cost of:
  - any disclosure directions sought; and
  - when seeking permission to rely on expert evidence;
- as case progresses amended budgets may be filed and approved, typically at CMC.
- At end of litigation, recoverable costs are assessed in accordance with approved budgets.

Pre-trial review [PRT]
- if needed takes place 8 to 10 weeks before trial. Court will:
- check compliance with earlier orders;
- explore settlement;
- make directions about conduct of trial, how evidence to be adduced and time limits on cross-examination etc.;
- parties may agree to vary case management timetable; where sanction for non-compliance Ps can agree a maximum 28-day extension, only if it does not **affect date set for 5 things:**
  - returning directions questionnaires

- cost management conference [CMC]*
- pre-trial review [PTR]*
- returning pre-trial checklists and
- trial date
- If any of these dates would be affected, permission of Court must be sought

Allocation
- Once case provisionally allocated to a track and directions questionnaires returned, judge will consider 3 things;
- if claim or defence should be stopped e.g. struck out or summary judgement
- formal track allocation;
- case management directions; given using a standard form adapted to individual needs and typical include:
- disclosure of documents;
- exchange of witness statements and expert evidence.
- Court is under a duty to further the overriding objective by actively managing cases which includes:
  - encouraging cooperation;
  - encouraging ADR;
  - controlling progress;
  - considering whether proposed steps justify the cost;
  - dealing efficiently with cases- sometimes without hearing
- **CPR 3 Powers and punishments include:**
- building punishments in to orders; "unless orders";
- making orders with conditions such as payment;
- making orders on its own initiative;
- contacting the parties to monitor compliance;
- imposing sanctions for non-compliance with directions and orders;
- extending or refusing to extend time;
- controlling nature and extent of evidence to be given at trial

3 matters Court disregard is decide to which track the claim should be allocated

Any amount not in dispute

intend

cost

contributory negligent.

75

Powers and sanctions

Striking out claims: CPR 3.4

- This is end of claim.
- Striking out statement of case means it is deleted; can no longer be relied on
  - If defence struck out, C entitled to default judgement- chapter 13
  - If default judgement against D after defence struck out, D may apply under CPR 3.6 for relief

The test; statement of case will be struck out if: CPR 3.4

- no reasonable grounds for bringing or defending claim e.g. bare denial
- it is abuse of court process
- has been failure to comply with rule/ PD/ court order

Abuse of process;

- Attempts to re-litigate decided issues and collateral attacks on early decisions
- Whether litigating decided case amounts to abuse of process depends on all circumstances including;
- all public interests and all private interests;
- further potential form of abuse is party attacking a final decision against them made by Court

Discretion;

- court has discretion when considering striking out and may
- allow party to amend their statement of case or
- treat application as one for summary judgement
- In case of non-compliance with rule/ PD/ court order, strikeout is a rare, extreme measure

Less draconian alternatives include:

- awarding costs on indemnity basis;
- ordering party pays money into Court;
- an unless order may be appropriate;

- statement of case should not be stuck out if contains disputed fact that can only be properly determined at hearing
- nor is it appropriate to strikeout pleading in developing area of law
Procedure; Application to strikeout:
- interim application made under CPR 23 chapter 12.2;
- usually made **with notice;**
- no evidence required but evidence usually filed and served;
- on application will usually be hearing;
- strikeout sought on basis **no reasonable grounds for bringing or defending claim;**
- hearing will assume facts in statement of case true;
- Courts can strike out at any stage (not only an interim remedy???) but should strike out early to save expense if possible, usually between an acknowledgement of service and directions questionnaire
- Sometimes strikeout is built in and sanction follows automatically after default:
  - to rules; e.g. non-payment of fees at track allocation stage;
  - to a Court order; e.g. unless order.
- Court considering strikeout should consider effect on P's rights to access to Court; important under art 6 ECHR
- Each case must be decided on its merits;
- To obtain judgement after strike out, innocent P just needs to file request;
- Court power to make orders consequential to order of striking including entering judgement CPR 3.4 (3)

Claims and applications totally without merit CPR 3.3 (7)
- If court of own initiative strikes out statement of case / dismisses application as **totally without merit;**
  - Court should record on court file that claim / application totally without merit;
  - Court must consider **civil restraint order;**

- In summary, restraint order is order preventing a person from engaging in litigation.

Other sanctions for non-compliance:

Power to impose sanctions for non-compliance are important to maintain control of litigation. Sanctions for non-compliance with:
Timetable directions:

- is minor default provided key case management events unaffected;
- Ps should seek to resolve, agreeing new date for compliance;
- innocent P should warn defaulting P of intention to make application to court if direction not complied with before making application for order to enforce compliance or sanction.
Pre-action default
- Non-compliance with pre-action protocols or PD PAC will not cause concern if minor;
- where unnecessary litigation results, costs sanctions can follow; costs or interest ordered as a punishment;
- Directions questionnaires ask if Ps have completed pre-action protocols so non-compliance should be no surprise
CPR contains other built-in sanctions, for example:
- CPR 35.13- if P fails to disclose expert evidence, P will not be able to rely on it, unless Court gives permission;
- rule-based section for failure to file / save costs budgets in time; Mitchell v News group newspapers Ltd;
- where sanction for non-compliances within rules, by written prior agreements Ps may give themselves extension of up to 28 days, provided no hearing date affected.

Relief from sanctions CPR 3.9:

- Ps can apply to court to grant relief from sanctions;
- where sanction built in to order as unless order, mandated by a rule or PD, it automatically takes effect unless; defaulting party applies for and is granted relief from sanction, CPR **3.9;**
- Court simply required to consider **all circumstances of case** to enable it to deal with application justly including

- need for litigation to be conducted **efficiently and at proportionate cost**; and
- to **enforce compliance with rules, PDs and orders**.
- Application must be supported by written evidence;
- **In Mitchell** Court of Appeal said applying 3.9 the court must
  - apply overriding objective and
  - carry out a balancing exercise where two most important factors of those listed in the rule:
    - o need for litigation to be conducted efficiently at proportionate cost; and
    - o to enforce compliance with rules, PDs and orders.
- Leading case; when relief from sanctions granted **Denton v White;** Court should consider application in 3 stages:
  - Identify and assess **seriousness** and significance of breach; if trivial, relief from sanction usually granted;
  - when non-compliance **significant**; court will consider **why** it occurred
  - Evaluate **all circumstances** of case, giving **priority to 2 factors** in CPR 3.9 above;
- Inefficiency or incompetence unlikely to be sufficient reason, circumstances outside P's control might be;
- **Mitchell gives examples of good and bad reasons for breach:**
- Good reasons:
  - P or solicitor has debilitating illness or in accident;
  - later developments demonstrate original time for compliance not reasonable
- Bad reason:
  - Solicitor overlooks deadline because of pressure of work
- **Decision in Denton:** decided to discourage opportunism by non-defaulting P;
- Ps should be ready to agree reasonable extensions of time or risk costs of application for relief from sanction;
- tolerance to non-compliance is low.

- Application for relief from sanction presupposes sanction properly imposed (if P contends Court wrong to make order it should appeal);
- If P needs more time to comply, P should apply for extension of time or Ps should agree extension under CPR 38.4,
- Applications for extension made before time has expired looked on more positively than those made later.
- Principles governing relief from sanction also apply to applications seeking imposition of sanctions.
- Only in exceptional circumstances will Court allow failing to comply with a direction or unless order to postpone trial
- Where action struck out for failure to comply with unless order, second claim brought on same basis would normally be struck out as abuse of process.
- Court should exercise its wide powers ensuring any penalty is commensurate with nature of default;
- any sanction which deprives P of access to Court such as striking out should be a sanction of last resort.

Extension of time and correcting irregularities:
- Court has general power to extend time to allow Ps to remedy procedural errors;
- power used in keeping with overriding objective and applications made in good time have best chance;
- power may not be used to renew invalid claim forms which have expired.

Applications to revoke or vary:
- Court has power to revoke or vary an order; does so sparingly where:
  - material change in circumstances; or
  - facts on which original order based were misstated; or
  - manifest mistake by Judge who made order

Stay:
- Rather like with a dog, stay produces temporary halt, it can become a permanent state;

- whilst stay place no other steps can be taken to progress claim;
- if C accepts offer in settlement, proceedings will be stayed, effectively ending case.

Stay for settlement [CPR 26.40]:

- on filing DQ, P may make written request to give Ps opportunity to settle;
- if all Ps agree, claim stayed;
- in absence of agreement, Court may order stay;
- length of stay; usually **1 month.**

Tomlin order (see chapter):

- special form of consent order;
- stays proceedings in any claim compromised except for purpose of putting into effect terms in schedule to order.

Discontinuance

- Something C does if, having commenced proceedings, decides to abandon them for whole or part of claim
- C serves notice of discontinuance on D, agreeing to pay costs.
- Permission of Court not required unless an order made or an aspect of case needs managing
- If discontinuance follows filing of a defence, a second claim brought on substantially the same facts would not be allowed without Court's permission

Read CPR 3.1—3.11 and PD 30 about the courts powers.

Small claims	FastTrack	Multitrack
NB: often without lawyers	*NB: Most PI claims*	*NB: complex cases*
Claims for £10 K, or less	MORE THAN >£10K claim to £25K	Claims > £25K
Pi claims where £1K or less, PSLA claimed	Where trial will last < one day Pi claims where +£1K PSLA claimed	All part 8 claims

Housing disrepair where Repairs £1 K, or less and Damages £1K, or less	Claim to expert evidence not exceed; • 2 expert fields • One expert per Field	All part 8 claims
	Claims for< £10 K involving disputed allegation of dishonesty	
DQ due within 14 days	DQ due within 28 days (after notice of provisional allocation)	ditto (28 days)

Features of tracks
Case Prep; typical directions small claims and fast-track:

Direction- DEExT	Small claims	Fast-track
Disclosure (& inspection)	Copies of all docs relied on **14 days** before hearing **Original docs** to be brought to hearing	Standard disclosure
Exchange of Witness statements	**May** be required having regard to • Amount • Whether Ps represented • Whether order for further info would bring clarity	**Always** required Service by simultaneous exchange
Experts	No expert report without permission	• Joint expert unless good reason • Usually no oral expert evidence
Special directions	May order a P to clarify their case	To confirm trial date and provide bundle

Sanctions re minor breaches;
- Court will allow P in breach limited time to comply and/or
- Court will make a costs order against P in breach

Likely sanctions for serious breaches:
- any revised deadline set by court will be final;
- serious breach may result in immediate imposition of sanctions;
- Court will make costs order against P in breach and / or Court may make "unless order"

Unless order;
- States **unless** P complies with specific step in specific time sanctions will apply;
- usually striking out of particulars of claim or defense
- Court will only make unless order if satisfied sanction appropriate
- P subject to unless order should **appeal unless order** rather than seeking relief from sanction- see chapter 23.6

Automatic sanctions;
- Some rules contain automatic sanctions; no application to court required for sanction to have effect e.g. CPR 32.10
- E.g.: If P failed to provide witness statement by specified time, P may not call witness to give oral evidence, unless court gives permission
- CPR 3.8 provides any sanction imposed by rule has effect, unless P in breach **claims relief from sanctions**

Time limits ;
- Normal rule; parties may vary time-limit specified by written agreement CPR 2.11
- Stricter rule where rule or order specifies sanction for non-compliance; CPR 3.8 (4) provides time for doing an act / ordered by Court can be extended by up to 28 days by prior written agreement of Ps subject proviso;
- extension does not put hearing date at risk

Power to rectify errors of procedure CPR 3.1:
- where error of procedure e.g. failure to comply with rule;
- error does not invalidate any step in proceedings unless court orders it;

- court may make order to remedy error

Summary:

- case management and cost management have significant role in litigation;
- by agreeing costs budgets Ps limit ability of Courts to intervene;
- strikeout extreme measure and Court reluctant to order as first resort.

***

CHAPTER 13

Disclosure, Inspection of Documents and Privilege
Definition CPR 31.2 and CPR 31.3

- After case allocated to track it enters second half of litigation process; period dominated by disclosure of documents;
- enables Ps to see case against them, narrow issues, even settle
- Following allocation, court gives track specific directions and disclosure usually ordered;
- Ps under continuing duty to disclose until proceedings conclude CPR 31.11.
- If privilege document accidentally released, inspecting P can only use with Court's permission
- On small claims track, disclosure usually limited to documents Ps intend to rely on at trial
- CPR rules aim to keep disclosure effective and proportionate.
- Use of disclosed documents restricted to the purposes of litigation in which they disclosed until in public domain, having been read in court, restriction then ends, unless Court orders otherwise;
- Court has discretion to sanction use of a document for a collateral purpose, even not in public domain.
- Fast-track and multitrack disclosure can take 2 routes:
  - standard disclosure: given in fast-track, multitrack PI claims and other multitrack claims where Court directs
  - menu option procedure: governs all other multitrack cases.

Standard disclosure:
- standard disclosure generally ordered at case allocation or case management conference;
- Ps disclose existence of every disclosable document they have or had in their possession or power;

- duty to disclose limited to documents which are or have been in his control CPR 31.8 (2); deemed where A:
- is or was in physical possession;
- has or had right to possession; or
- has or had right to inspect and take copies of it;
- usually done by exchange of disclosure lists;
- Ps must allow one other to inspect documents still in their possession which are not privileged or protected;
- Disclosure is 2 stage process:
- disclosure by list;
- inspection;
- once written notice of request given inspection should be permitted **within 7 days;**
- inspection can take place by viewing documents or sending photocopies;
- there is a right to request photocopies if reasonable costs are paid;
- inspection can take place electronically, what is appropriate varies from case to case;
- Standard disclosure requires P to disclose only documents on which he relies and
  - which could adversely affect his case or other P's case;
  - support other P's case; and
  - required by any practice direction;
- this does not include documents relevant only to credibility.
- Adversely effects; not defined but fact specific.
- **Harrods v Times newspapers;** confirms document which may provide a line of enquiry is insufficient to amount to having an adverse effect;
- standard disclosure can be limited or dispensed with by written agreement of Ps or Court order, for example where disclosure has already taken place;
- Ps may not agree to widen ambit of disclosure, only Court can do this.

Menu Option disclosure:
- some multitrack cases so complex standard disclosure could involve huge number of documents;
- menu option gives scope for proportionate orders on case-by-case basis;
- in none PI multitrack claims, menu option applies unless court orders otherwise, with 3 stages:
  1   Disclosure report
- Ps must file and serve <u>disclosure reports</u> not less than **14 days before first CMC;**
- verified by statement of truth;
- describing relevant documents, where are they are and cost of disclosing; (must reconcile with Ps cost budgets);
- should summarise any disclosure directions sought.
  2   Agreed proposal for directions
- Ps must seek to agree disclosure proposal for Court not less than **7 days before CMC**;
- may meet in person or by telephone;
- any proposal agreed must be filed with Court;
- Court may approve proposal without hearing, saving expense
  3   CMC disclosure direction
- if Court wishes to have hearing, will be at CMC, choosing from the menu of disclosure options
- options include:
  - standard disclosure;
  - specific disclosure (see below);
  - each P disclose documents it relies on and requests disclosure it requires;
  - disclosure by each P on issue by issue basis;
  - Court make any other order it thinks fit or dispense with further disclosure
- Court should make any order having regard to overriding objective; need to act proportionately, limiting disclosure to what is necessary;
- Court may also give directions about how disclosures to given.
  Key points for disclosure in all cases include:

- documents can include anything; paper, discs, video and audio recordings;
- P's duty to disclose limited to documents which are or have been in his control;
- disclosing P must make <u>reasonable search</u> for all disclosable documents according to case needs; **CPR 31.7**
- Reasonableness determined by ref to:
- number of docs;
- nature and complexity of proceedings;
- ease and expense of doc retrieval;
- significance of docs;
- what is reasonable varies according to circumstances and the overriding principle of proportionality;
- D automatically acquires rights to inspect document except where:
- document no longer under A's Control;
- D has legal duty to withhold inspection e.g. privilege; or
- A considers it disproportionate to issues in the case to permit inspection.
- <u>disclosure statement</u> must be included confirming
  - understanding of and compliance with duty to disclose and
  - extent of search or why not reasonable to search for documents;
  - normally be signed by Ps personally (it is their responsibility to make full disclosure)
- Exchange list sets out disclosable documents in 3 sections; documents that documents P1;
  - still has;
  - still has but which P2 may not see; privilege documents existence must be disclosed but usually vaguely;
  - no longer has.
- P may ask at any time to see document mentioned in a statement of case, witness statement, affidavit, or expert witness report. Inspection can follow immediately
- Court can limit inspection or agree inspection may be disproportionate to case and need not take place

Specific disclosure or inspection:

- P may identify document or class of documents missing from list in application to Court for disclosure or inspection;
- can be made at any stage; but later more likely to carry costs, best if court giving other directions e.g. at CMC
- application on notice; under CPR 23 using an application notice
- should specify:
- order sought;
- reason applicant believes document should be disclosed.
- When considering application court has regard to;
  - overriding objective\ and
  - proportionality
- underlying rationale is that CPR 1.1 requires A to get access to all docs which may assist B case, confirmed in Commissioners of Inland Revenue v Exeter City AFC
- CPR 31.1 protects B
- CPR 31.19 provides opportunity for A to make pre-emptive application;
  - permission to withhold disclosure/ inspection on public interest grounds
  - HC and CC retain parallel jurisdiction re search and application; S 35 Senior Courts act and S 54 CC Act
- Penalty for nondisclosure may include P in default not relying on document without trial Judge permission

Exceptional disclosure orders against non P; kind of pre-action disclosure

Norwich Pharmacal; common-law procedure to get disclosure of identity of wrongdoers

- Lord Reid;

  "If a person gets mixed up in the transactions of others to facilitate their wrongdoing

  he comes under a duty to assist the person who has been wronged by giving full information and disclosing the identity of the wrongdoer"

- typical witness has no such duty and cannot be compelled to disclose what they saw until trial;

Relief via Norwich Pharmacal order helpfully summarised in Mitsui:

- wrong must have been committed by wrongdoer;
- need for order must exist to enable action to be brought against wrongdoer;
- 3rd-party must:
- have facilitated wrongdoing; and
- be able to provide info necessary to enable wrongdoer to be sued.
- Norwich Pharmacal orders only available in High Court because they derive from its jurisdiction;
- not limited to disclosure of documents, can include answering questions;
- remedy is discretionary;
- information sought must not be protected by privilege;
- kind of pre-action disclosure because until name of wrong-doer known, no action can be brought against him;
- appropriate where P knows he has good claim against someone but doesn't know who;
- facilitator supplies missing piece of jigsaw.

Procedure for making Norwich Pharmacal application

- If facilitator innocent
- interim application made;
- issues claim form against facilitator seeking disclosure of identity of wrongdoer;
- to High Court
- on notice, unless urgency or secret C justifies not doing so
- once identity of wrongdoer disclosed, proceedings end
- If claimant also suing facilitator, who is not innocent
  - application made as interim application in that action

- applicant pays cost of application but it may be recovered from wrongdoer at end of case

Statutory pre-action disclosure
- available in HC and CC;
- appropriate where A know who D is but unsure case strong enough to be worthwhile;
- Court has power to make order for disclosure of;
  - material documents where;
  - R and A likely to be Ps to subsequent proceedings
  - available against future D whose identity known and
  - early disclosure will save costs or encourage settlement
- applications are an interim application in the anticipated litigation (may sound strange);
- disclosure limited to documents normally disclosable in litigation;
- no need to show claim likely to be brought, just that if it were, applicant and respondent likely parties
- Court will not look deeply into merits;
- application determined in keeping with overriding objective;
- Court has discretion to refuse order.

- Pre-action disclosure differs from Norwich Pharmacal as
  - statutory
  - limited to disclosure of documents which would be subject to standard disclosure
  - applicant knows who D would be, just does not know if case worth pursuing
- Costs usually bourn by P seeking order unless Court finds R forced an unnecessary application, then may award costs to applicant.

Orders against stranger to ongoing litigation
- As an exception to general rule that disclosure can only be brought against Ps to proceedings;
- once case commences, P may get order for production of relevant documents by stranger to litigation;
- where non-P has control of documents likely to help applicant's case;
- not a form of pre-action disclosure;
- application made by:

- Part 23 interim application in ongoing proceedings (or on Court's own initiative)
- as with pre-action disclosure, rules do not support fishing expeditions
- on notice;
- supported by written evidence;
- order must specify what documents to be disclosed;
- can ask respondent to indicate where documents are, if no longer in his possession or control.

Inspection of relevant property
- Objects can provide evidential information; called relevant property; **Order giving one-P access to relevant things in possession of another P;**
- normally available only against parties' litigation, but there are exceptions;
  - In normal course of litigation: if machine injures P it is relevant property and order would allow for preservation of machine and access to it
  - analogous situation is seeking order for medical examination of person injured
  - As C is human, Court cannot force C to do this but Court can achieve same outcome by ordering halt to proceedings, if C unreasonably refuses medical examination;
  - order granted at discretion of Court
- Sometimes came into anyone into subject next to medical examination conditions for example the presence of friends, many are uncontroversial
- Condition which interfere the purpose of the examination maybe considered unreasonable
- Application for such orders; to gain access to inspect things people or are:
  - made on notice;
  - supported by written evidence which speaks to need and relevance of order
  - often unnecessary as Ps willing to give access

Exceptional orders

- two statutory exceptions re disclosure of documents;
- <u>Where an object may become relevant to subject matter of subsequent</u> proceedings, is possible to get order for inspection etc. before proceedings start;
- possible to get such orders against a non-P if he is in control of property relevant to subject matter of litigation:
    - o Application generally made on notice
    - o supported by a written evidence
    - o identifying property in question and need for order
- ***Pre-action disclosure [PAD] CPR 31.16;***
- *Prospective P to proceedings may apply to court for disclosure of docs*
- *using part 23 application notice*
- *rules prohibit fishing ;*
- *application must be precise and limited to what strictly necessary;*
- *Conditions for pre-action disclosure;*
- *Respondent likely to be P to subsequent proceedings and*
- *Applicant likely to be P to proceedings and*
- *hypothetically, standard disclosure would apply to doc applicant seeking and*
- *disclosure before issuing proceedings desirable to;*
- *dispose fairly of anticipated proceedings or*
- *help dispute resolution or*
- *save costs*
- *In assessing whether ordering pre-action disclosure is desirable court takes a **two stage process;***
- *Jurisdictional; Address is whether real prospect of order being **fair** to Ps, and*
- *discretionary; based on court assessment of facts.*
- *In assessing merits of future claim courts require P to show prima facie entitlements to substantive relief*
- *Costs of pre-action disclosure - special case under CPR 46.1*

- *General rule; person against whom order sought pay costs of application and of complying with order*

Privilege

- 2 types of privilege:
  - privilege against self-incrimination; and
  - legal professional privilege which takes two forms; legal advice privilege and litigation privilege;

  (privilege is personal and may only be waived by person protected)
- also protection of without prejudice communications, not strictly privilege, only be waived by all parties protected;
- public interest immunity is not privilege but imposes a duty to withhold disclosure:
  - obliges Courts to exclude evidence on ground disclosure would damage public interest;
  - obligation cannot be waived by anybody.

Privilege against self-incrimination:

- Protects person from being compelled by state to give incriminating evidence against himself

Legal professional privilege [LPP]

A   Legal advice privilege [LAP]:

- confidential communication between legal adviser and client (or person representing clients) in connection with giving / receiving legal advice is protected by LPP;
- covers all legal advice / assistance between client and lawyer regardless of whether litigation contemplated;
- communication in connection with crime or fraud are exceptions to principle;
- reason for LAP; in public interest that people feel able to seek legal advice in complete confidence
- only client can waive privilege;
- lawyer must be qualified; not include specialist tax accountant giving legal advice (Prudential, 2013)

- Communication between 3rd party and lawyer not protected by LAP
  B   Litigation privilege:
- involves a third party;
- confidential communication between legal advisor and/ or his client and third party are privilege where:
- dominant purpose in communicating or creating document is;
- to obtain legal advice or help in conduct of litigation reasonably in prospect;
- for example, an expert's report;
- the test provides that provided:
  - right person; person commissioning the document;
  - has right motivation; litigation;
  - is immaterial whether litigation takes place;
- Rationale is, P should be free to conduct litigation confidentially;
- if document came into existence before litigation reasonably in prospect, privilege does not extend to document;
- P need not produce such documents for inspection at disclosure stage:
- can be useful if P receives unfavourable report from experts;
- if P does not want to rely on such privileged document he can throw it away.
  Waiver of legal professional privilege:
- LPP belongs to and can only be waived by client;
- waiver can be express or implied;
- sometimes advice can be important to explain to Court behavior of client or adviser;
- question may arise about extent to which privilege can be waived and usually determined objectively; occasionally disclosure trumps confidentiality and can amounts to waver of all privileged advice material.
- **Cable& Wireless; authority for proposition when determining what constitutes waiver:**
1) Court will consider what has been disclosed by P; and
2) circumstances in which disclosed;
3) fairness remains overriding principle in context of disclosure

Without prejudice communication:

- private without prejudice communication made in genuine attempt to settle disputes are protected from disclosure to trial Court;
- protection for both sides equally and can only be waived if both sides agree;
- aim: to encourage negotiation and remove fear (that admissions in negotiation may be used at trial);
- test looks at substance rather than form of communication:
- posting "without prejudice" on documents does not guarantee protection;
- document may be protected when not marked "without prejudice";
- purpose behind communication is what matters.
- the protection extends to negotiations which fail

Public interest immunity [PII]:

- documents must be withheld from disclosure and inspection if revealing their:
- existence; and/ or
- contents;
- would injure public interest;
- public interest immunity is a duty not privilege;
- for Court in each instance to decide where public interest lies;
- Court balances public interest in concealment against public interest in fair and open justice;
- PII claims can be made without notice and any order made must not, unless Court orders otherwise, be served on any other person.
- PII applies to both disclosure and inspection, unlike LPP which prevents inspection but not disclosure.

Exceptions:

- without prejudice communication that lead to settlement are admissible for purposes of proving the settlement; and

- communication "without prejudice save as to costs" is admissible for purpose of assessing costs;
- without prejudice protection attaches from date of production of document and applies in all proceedings;
- wrongly using without prejudice document at trial may lead to:
- abortive trial and / or
- wasted costs order.

Summary:
- disclosure and inspection is two stage process;
- standard disclosure rules not used for non-PI multitrack cases;
- Ps under continuing duty of disclosure.

***

CHAPTER 14

Interim Applications – Part 23.

- Most cases settle before trial, for this reason civil course focuses on events in interim period.
- Issuing claim form starts interim period, it continues until trial.
- Called interlocutory period.
- P may need to ask Court for order prior to trial; known as interim application.
- Interim applications should be made as soon as possible.

CPR Part 23 sets out general rules about interim applications.

- In HC most interim applications made to Master; procedural judge with no significant trial jurisdiction.
- Some interim applications must be made to HC judge, e.g.: injunctions.
- In CC, equivalent of Master is District Judge, who hears most interim applications.
- Applications which District Judge cannot hear are made to Circuit Judge.
- District Judge has some trial jurisdiction, where claim not more than £25k and can grant injunctions in such cases.

Most Part 23 interim applications made:

- using **Application Notice**; official form which must contain or be accompanied by:
- description of order sought;
- reasons why A seeking order;
- supported by written evidence including witness statements; and be
- in writing;
- on notice;
- filed at court and served on all Ps at least 3 clear days before hearing;

[the "return date"- everyone returns to court to hear application]

- including draft order sought (on disk as well as hardcopy, if complex so easy to adapt).
  [Rule, PD or court order may dispense with requirement of application notice]

- <u>Any evidence in reply</u> should be filed and served as soon as possible thereafter.
- More complex applications involve longer notice period; see summary judgement and interim payments
- Interim applications can be made without notice:
  - out of **necessity**- if no defendant on record;
  - because matter so **urgent** there is no time; or
  - where **secrecy** vital;
- any interim order without notice should make provision for return date, where both A and R may make submissions;
- if made without notice applicant under duty to make **"full and frank"** disclosure of all material facts: golden rule;
- obligation to compensate for other side's absence, not exploit it;
- sanctions for failure can be severe:
  - R may make application to discharge injunction on basis of **material nondisclosure;**
  - **Brink's Mat**; confirms, R can only bring such application with proper reason, not dubious grounds
  - If R succeeds, question of fresh application may arise.
  - Judge must undertake balancing exercise of A and R's interests and general approach of Courts is to deter others from not adhering to golden rule

Written evidence must be provided:
- in notice of application, if it contains a statement truth;
- in any statement of case, if it contains a statement of truth
- in a witness statement, including a statement of truth to be served with application notice; or
- in an affidavit, to be served with application notice.

Note: affidavit costs more than witness statement due to cost of being sworn;
litigant will not generally recover cost of making affidavit;
for this reason, most interim applications supported by witness statements.

- Rules encourage dealing with interim applications on papers; without Ps attending hearing;
- serves overriding objective by saving time and money.
- Urgent application usually dealt with at hearing, in extreme urgency, may be dealt with by telephone.
- Application may be dealt with without hearing where:
  - P agree terms of order; or
  - application should be disposed of without hearing; or
  - Court considers it inappropriate to hold hearing
- General rule; hearing in public;
- Judge may order hearing in private in exceptional circumstances
- Court's case management powers are wide and include:
  - conducting hearings by telephone; and
  - making orders where no one has asked.
- More complicated the matter, more likely counsel instructed, skeleton arguments filed and exchanged etc.
- Disputes of fact in interim applications are a challenge as lack of oral testimony or opportunity to test evidence:
  - disputes of fact decided by asking applicant if he has established a "good arguable case";
  - amounts to claimant saying "Court should be as satisfied as it can be in the circumstances", given limitations of hearing based on written evidence and wanting to avoid mini trials.
- If interim application takes less than a day (normal), Court normally makes summary assessment of costs then.

Set aside / vary / stay
- P unhappy with determination of interim hearing can apply to have decision set aside / varied / stayed

General rule; Application notice must be served on each R - PD 23A (3);

- **Without notice application** may be warranted if good reason for not giving notice such as:
  - urgency of remedy sought; or
  - confidentiality; or
  - where court order, rule or PD permits;
- Court usually expects A to informally notify R where formal notice not given.
- Once order made without notice, A under duty to serve R with all relevant documents for hearing.
- If application to court before issue of application, A has to issue a claim form immediately or Court will give directions re commencement of claim:
  - where court order made and application notice not served on R prior to being made;
  - R may apply to have order set aside or varied within **7 days** of being served with the order

Where to make Part 23 application CPR 23.2

- General rule; application for interim remedy made to court where claim issued
- If claims since transferred; application made to transfer court, unless good reasons otherwise

When application made CPR 23.5

- Application made when application notice received by Court within the specified time

Dismissal of totally without merit application CPR 23.12

- Where Court dismisses application and considers application **totally without merit must records fact in order** and
- Consider whether civil restraint order appropriate.

Periods of notice in interim applications PD 23A 3A (4.1-4.2)

- Application notice must be served as soon as possible after issue;
- if to be hearing, application notice must be served at least **3 clear days** before hearing;

- where application notice should be served but insufficient time, **informal notification** of application should be given, unless circumstances of application require secrecy

Summary:
- CPR 23 application normal way of making an interim application to court:
- usually heard in public;
- application notice served **three clear days** prior;
- where application without notice, A usually expected to inform R informally.

***

CHAPTER 15A

Interim Payments and Security for Costs

- Interim payments - sought by C against D
- Security for costs - usually sought by D (against a C - unless CC)

Interim Payments

- Interim payments help C during long period until trial or assessment of damages.
- Potential benefits to D too; if injured C uses money for rehabilitation, may reduce claim and interest liability.
- C gets some of money remedy on account before trial, damages, debt, other sum (except costs);
- application cannot be made before time D given to acknowledge service;
- Court may order D to make an interim payment to C where:
  - D admitted liability; or
  - C has judgement against D, damages to be assessed; e.g. default or summary judgement, or
  - Court satisfied if claim went to trial C would obtain judgement for **substantial damages** from D
- Substantial means: **not negligible or nominal**, judged in overall context of case;
- means interim payment inappropriate for most small claims cases and most made in multitrack cases.
- Standard of proving claim would succeed is **balance of probabilities**
- Court has discretion but if conditions made out an order is usually made, unless good reason not to.
- An interim payment has no cost implications

McArdle decided:

- C does not have to show need for money as precondition;
- but PD requires C to include in supporting evidence what money will be used for

Multiple Ds - where two or more Ds:

- if clear an individual D will be liable to C, court can order interim payment against that D,
- if unclear which D the C will succeed against, interim payments may still be ordered if establish:
  - C will succeed against at least one named D, and
  - all Ds either insured, public bodies or D's liability will be met
  [Where insurance companies and public bodies involved no great injustice if one D has to reimburse another]

How much

- Interim payment must not exceed a **reasonable portion** of likely amount of final judgement;
- rules no more specific and allow exercise of discretion;
- counterclaims, set offs and contributory negligence must be taken into account

If interim payment ordered, no mention should be made to trial judge until liability and quantum are decided,

- unless D agrees;
- risk of prejudice if trial judge knows interim judge thought case favoured C;
  - if rule forgotten could result in:
  - mis-trial; or
  - personal costs order.

Procedure

- Fairly typical part 23 interim application;
- application for interim payment cannot be made before time D given to acknowledge service
- like **summary judgement application**; application must be served on D **at least 14 clear days before hearing**;
- D should serve any evidence in reply **at least 7 days before hearing;**
- any further evidence in reply from C must be filed **at least 3 days before hearing.**
- made on notice;
- with supporting evidence;
- in writing including;

- amount sought;
- **what payment will be used for;**
- **expected total judgement;**
- reasons for believing grounds made out;
- documents in support must be included including medical reports;
- in PI claim, detail of special damages and past and future loss and
- in claims under Fatal Accidents Act, details of person on whose behalf claim made and nature of claim;
- in PI cases should obtain and file <u>certificate of recoverable benefits.</u>
Effect of set-offs and counterclaims CPR 25.7 (5)
- Once principle of interim order decided, Court moves to second stage; quantum;
- take into account set-off or CC and any contributory negligence;
- Counterclaims affect amount of final award likely, if CC worth more than claim, interim payment not appropriate;
- set offs are also defences and go to first stage of court's decision; grounds for granting the order;
- if set-off has reasonable prospects of success, Court may not be satisfied C will obtain judgement against D
Powers of Courts following order CPR 25.8;
Having made an order for D to make interim payment Court has power to
- adjust figure, ordering interim payment repaid, part or full; or
- discharge order; or
- order reimbursement between multiple Ds

***

CHAPTER 15B

Security for Costs

- D may be confident he will defeat a claim but concerned C as loser may be unable to meet an order for costs
- Only some Ds can get protection against this
- Award is discretionary
- A typical order in QBD requires C to:
- pay specific amount of money in to court;
- as security for payment of any costs order made in favour of D;
- staying C's claim until security given.
   There are 2 hurdles:
- C must fall in a very narrow class;
- Court must be satisfied having regard to all the circumstances it is just do so,

First hurdle (if D cannot pass first hurdle, no security for costs possible):
- C is ordinarily resident outside domestic but not resident in a European jurisdiction, or
   [Note: D carries burden of proof. Rationale: ability to pay costs of concern where C's assets are foreign]
- C is an impecunious company
   - *Note: must be reason to believe C unable to pay D's costs;*
   - *evidence needed includes proof C is in insolvency proceedings or signed witness statement of C's inability to pay*

Second hurdle
- Court satisfied with regards to all the circumstances it is just to do so.
   Every case will be determined on its individual facts:
- Rule not more specific and might include?
   - are there special difficulties enforcing a cross order?

- is it obvious merits favour one side (without conducting mini trial)?
- how clear is it D will win and get costs?
- can D recover costs from anyone else?
- impact of award on C?
- did D contribute to C's financial difficulty;
- did D delay making application?

Procedure

- Usual Part 23 procedure applies
- application normally made first CMC;
- on notice;
- to master or district judge;
- application notice must be served on C **at least 3 clear days before hearing**;
- supported by written evidence;
- setting out basis of application;
- factors relevant to Court's discretion; and
- estimate of likely costs of defending claim

Size of order

- Amount security ordered within Court's discretion;
- should not be oppressive;
- often security of 2/3rds costs up to stage of proceedings to which security ordered; often in future;
- common to award security in stages, as case may settle;
- an order for costs must specify how and when security must be given;

Joint claimants

- Court has discretion;
- Order made will depend on all the circumstances and;
- confidence Court has D will recover his costs;
- may be possible to get an award against 1 foreign Cs if 2 Cs and not relying on same cause of action or if each C will be responsible for his own share of D's costs all

Counterclaims:

1. unlike interim payments, order made against person in position of C

2. Means order for Security for Costs may be sought by:
    -   D in standard claim; or
    -   C, when D has counterclaimed

    Question of who pays costs not usually addressed until claim determined

    ***

CHAPTER 16

Interim injunction

Court may order interim relief either where:

- obvious C will win and unjust not to grant some of ultimate remedy pre-trial; or
- irreparable damage may be caused to C;
  interim payments and Interim injunctions are this kind of pre-trial order;
  interim versions of the kind of substantive remedy C ultimately seeks.

Interim injunctions are:

- temporary orders;
- granted by Court to regulate position between Ps pending trial:
  - mandatory injunction requires respondent to do defined act;
  - prohibitory injunction restrains respondent from specified conduct.
- Failure to obey is contempt of court; orders and consequences of breach are serious therefore applications made to:
  - High Court or Circuit judge (not Master or District judge); unless
  - case within District Judge's limited CC trial jurisdiction (£25k); or
  - Ps agree.
- Application must be founded on an identified course of action over which court has jurisdiction;
- **quia timet injunction** may be granted to prevent future wrong threatened; but C has to prove:
  - **high probability** of breach and
  - likelihood of **substantial damage**.
- occasionally, where **some,** not all, Ds are unknown, interim injunction granted against "persons unknown"

- As with all forms of equitable relief, whether or not to grant injunction is at Court's discretion;
- injunctions are a remedy not a right.
- Assuming application made on notice and both sides present, judge asked to make decision on written evidence;
- no testing of oral evidence, as would be at trial;
- makes decision on limited, written information about relief which may cause damage;
- for this reason, as long as there is serious issue to be tried, action is not frivolous or vexatious, decision is reached on the **balance of convenience;**
- Generally, A required to give a cross undertaking to compensate for any loss suffered by D as result of injunction.

Which party would experience more irreparable hardship:
Leading guidance from **American Cyanamid v Ethicon** says:
- detailed examination of merits of case ought to be left to trial; only in special circumstances, as last resort, should Court consider substantive merits.
- Court should ask itself:

1. Is there a serious issue to be tried?
- Low hurdle; to satisfy Court cause of action has some substance;
- does not matter whether chances of success 30% or 70%;
- if no serious issues to be tried (chance of success 0%), injunction will be refused

2. Would C be adequately compensated in damages?
- Injunctions are equitable remedies and should not be awarded if damages would adequately compensate C;
- important to consider D's ability to pay, with this question;
- if damages would be adequate remedy for C and D could pay, injunction likely to be refused;
- if damages would not be adequate remedy, court will look at same issue from D's perspective:

3. Would D be adequately protected by undertaking in damages?

- An <u>undertaking in damages</u> is required when interim injunction is granted;
- promise by C to compensate D and other relevant person for loss caused by injunction if wrongly granted;
- if money would put D right, and C could pay damages awarded, normally injunction will be granted.

If damages not adequate for either P, court will look at:

4. Balance of convenience

- All other relevant factors considered to decide if injunction would cause "un-compensatable damage" to one side;
- might include; loss of job; loss of goodwill; public interest issues; length of time to trial etc. - *things money can't easily buy*

If scales still evenly balanced, court may ask:

5. What order best preserves serve status quo?

- In Cyanamid Lord Diplock said:
  "Where other factors appear evenly balanced it is a counsel of prudence… to preserve the status quo"
- Status quo; state of affairs before conduct complained of unless;
- unreasonable delay in which case it is state of affairs immediately before injunction;
- C must act promptly to prevent D's offending behavior of becoming status quo;
- **As a last resort court should consider the substantive merits;**
- Very rarely will court be justified in considering merits of the case in detail
- If this aspect of the case is clear it could go on the scales with everything else
- American Cyanamid guidance is applied flexibly to give effect to the overriding objective

Exceptions to American Cyanamid approach - Important know where Cyanamid test does not apply

2 situations where court will decide interim injunction on **apparent strength of cause of action; where**

- **facts not disputed, law clear** and applying one to the other is easy
  - court happy to **decide matter on merits** as obvious whom they favour. Trial unnecessary ("happy merits").
- **may never be trial because decision at interim stage amount to final outcome;**
  - court will decide matter on the merits but less happily ("sad merits")
  - sometimes outcome of interim application may make future consideration pointless;
  - E.g.; when **something due to happen soon**; it will be stopped or not depending on interim application;
  - unlikely to be later trial on issue or later trial may come too late to help.

Where court exceptionally decides application on its merits, must be far more than serious issue to be tried;

- C must have an **overwhelming case**
- C rarely can do this in sad merit situation - makes them feel sad too, when they lose.

Some exceptions to American Cyanamid;
Freedom of speech; Defamation

- Injunction to restrain alleged **defamation** (only) will not be granted where D intends to plead **justification;**
- or if granted without notice, will be discharged;
- unless alleged libel is obviously untrue.
- This is an historic exception to protect freedom of speech;
- public interest in freedom of speech takes priority over personal rights to protect reputation by injunction.
  Individual left his remedy in damages. [Does not include trademark infringement]

Freedom of speech and Article 10 EC HR. S12 (3) HRA 1998;

- C must show case which will **probably succeed** at trial before interim injunction granted;

- involves consideration of **merits of case** and is an adaptation of American Cyanamid.

Mandatory injunctions:
- likely to cause greater inconvenience then prohibitory therefore usually harder to get;
- More likely to cause irredeemable prejudice; National Commercial Bank of Jamaica;
- much depend on circumstances of case, Lord Hoffmann made clear in National Commercial Banks Jamaica Ltd

Procedure
- D may not apply for interim injunction unless D has filed an AoS or defence;
- application under CPR Part 23;
- may be made in any sort of case, even small claims;
- usually with notice;
- appropriate form issued and filed and served on other side at least **three clear days** before hearing;
- should attach draft order, unless case simple;
- supported by written evidence;
- skeleton arguments usually required, especially in HC;
- **costs schedule** should be filed by both sides **24 hours** before hearing;
- only justification for interim injunction without notice is **urgency;**
- where application made without formal notice all reasonable attempts should be made to tell other side;
- claim form should be issued unless case so urgent no time;
- in absence of other side; full and frank disclosure must be made;
- must explain why formal notice not given and what done to give informal notice;
- applicant should make note of hearing;
- order granted without notice will last a limited time, for application to be resumed after proper notice;
- order lasts only **until return date** when further hearing; Ps will make submissions re continuation / discharge of interim injunction;

- if R offers undertakings that A accepts, Ps should be clear whether interim injunction discharged or adjourned.

Relevant undertakings are important
- More undertakings required if application pre-action or without notice and include normal;
    - undertaking as to damages; and
    - undertaking to serve order on respondent;
- may also be necessary to give an undertaking to:
    - issue and serve claim form;
    - serve notice of application;
    - serve evidence on which application based;
  [In summary; what applicant unable to do for lack of time he must undertake to do as part of order granted.]
- Draft orders are in standard form and reflect the distinction; between urgent and non-urgent cases.

***

CHAPTER 17

Offers

- Part 36 encourages parties to settle, early;
  - where formal offer to settle made by C or by D;
  - before or after claim commenced;
  - where relief sought is money or not; and
  - also in respect of appeals;
  - does not apply to small claims track.
- **Part 36 offer by D: can be made at any stage**;
- D must make formal Part 36 offer to settle:
- in writing;
- say pursuant to CPR 36;
- specifying,
  - **not less than 21 days,** within which D liable for C's costs if accepts
  - *[failing to specify relevant period of not less than 21 days is serious defect; disqualifies Part 36 offer]*;
  - whether relates to whole or part claim;
  - whether takes account of counter claim;
- must be sufficiently certain to form contract; C should be able to determine what offer relates to and if necessary;
  - seek clarification in first instance from offeror; and
  - make application to Court, if necessary;
- indicate whether in full and final settlement; and
- offer single sum of money (for money claims), payable within 14 days of acceptance;
- D can increase offer at any time.
- Offer made when served on other P; a prescribed method of service should be used.
- If C legally represented, service must be on legal representative;
- offer treated as including all interest up to end of 21-day relevant period;

- for a stated period called relevant period of
    o   at least 21 days; or
    o   up to end of trial, if offer made less than 21 days before trial starts

- **If C accepts within 21 days, all proceedings stayed;**
- acceptance must be in writing;
- D pays C's costs to that point;
- If C rejects and cases goes to trial, trial judge will not know about offer until liability and quantum determined
- If at end of trial:
    -   outcome for C better than offer, costs follow the even as normal; D pays C's costs
    -   outcome for C same as or worse than D's offer; C must pay all costs incurred after offer made.
- counter offer does not extinguish earlier offer;
- Part 36 offer can be worded to expire automatically after the initial period
- otherwise, only formal written withdrawal takes offer off table

Exceptionally, permission of court required to accept Part 36 offer where:
- C is child;
- C acting under a legal disability;
- multiple Ds; and
- trial has started

Acceptance of offers by C – 4 options:

1. First 21 days
- C accepts offer, C entitled to 100% standard-base costs to date of service of notice of acceptance
- **before expiry of relevant period**, part 36 offer may only be withdrawn or terms changed with Court permission provided offeree has not served notice of acceptance, or
- if he accepted, offeror's application must be made within **7 days** of acceptance or before first day of trial, it earlier

2. After 21 days but before trial:

- if offer not time-limited or withdrawn, C can still accept offer, subject to Ps agreeing costs;
- usual outcome; D entitled to costs from end of 21-day period to date of acceptance;
- if Ps cannot agree, court will make this cost order, unless unjust to do so.
- After initial 21-days, D may withdraw offer or make new offer by serving new written notice; no permission required.
- Withdrawn offer cannot give rise to cost sanctions under Part 36 but can be taken into account when deciding final cost orders; Court has wide discretion

3. During trial two conflicting issues:
- C needs Court permission to accept P36 offer once trial starts [*as may be unjust to allow C to accept offer he had ignored when his case starts to go badly*];
- trial judge must not know about P36 offers until case over, unless Ps agree in writing;
- if all Ps agree in writing for trial judge to deal with matter; he judge decides [rule does not apply to interim applications (as eventual trial judge does not hear them)]
- otherwise C must apply to another judge;
- Court's discretion is unfettered but in most cases acceptance is granted;
- if acceptance allowed, usual rule; C recovers costs to end of initial 21-day period, D recovers costs thereafter;
- if inadvertent disclosure of P36 offer, for Judge to decide, considering all circumstances, whether carrying on with trial would be just.

If C never accepts offer
- C must obtain judgement better than P36 offer to avoid cost penalty;
- for money claims, C must recover more money, however small the difference such as 1p;
- if C obtains judgements equal or less than D's offer, usual order;
  - C gets costs to end of initial 21-day period;
  - thereafter C pays D's costs, unless such order is unjust.

- Sometimes called **split order**; D pays Cs costs to certain point after which roles reverse;
- this can be very expensive; trial costs potentially consuming all of C's damages

Sanctions in P36 will not apply, when:

- Court considers it unjust; Court retains wide discretion;
- offer formally withdrawn;
- offer reduced to make it less advantageous and less advantageous offer beaten;
- Part 36 offer not properly formulated;
- offer made less than 21 days before trial, unless Court disregards this.

D can also make Part 36 offers in non-money claims:

- process is same;
- challenging is to determine if judgement is more advantageous than an offer;
- Court looks at case in the round; taking into account circumstances.

Part 36 offer by C

- Cs encouraged to make part 36 offers;
- Procedure re offer and acceptance same as above;
- main difference is consequence to D of not accepting C's offer.
- If C's offer not accepted and C's trial outcome is equal to or better than C's offer:

[unless it thinks it unjust court will order D to pay]

- punitive **interest** on damages (not exceeding 10% above base rate) for from date 21-day period expired
- punitive **costs**, for period after 21-day period expired and
- **interest** on punitive costs (not exceeding 10% above base rate)
- an **additional amount** not exceeding £75,000 calculated as follows

In money claims additional amount is:

- 10% of first £500,000 damages; plus
- 5% above £500,000 up to £1m damages (i.e.: £75,000 max).

In non-money claims calculation based on costs:

- 10% of first £500,000 costs; plus
- 5% of next £500,000 costs awarded to C.
  Additional amount:
- encourages Cs to make sensible P36 offers;
- punishes Ds who do not accept;
- proportionality determines order Court finally makes and Court will also consider whether any offer was a genuine attempt to settle proceedings

Calderbank offers:
- written offer marked "without prejudice save as to costs"; or
- "without prejudice" with express reservation of right to refer to document re costs;
- consequence of Calderbank offers, Court can consider offer exercising its discretion re costs;
- a P36 offer that fails the procedural requirements CPR 36 can qualify as Calderbank offer.

Formal or technical defect with P36 offers:
- provided cause no real uncertainty or other prejudice to offeree Court may order usual Pt 36 consequences follow.

Costs must be determined by Court unless agreed by Ps, where Pt 36 offer:
- made less than 21 days before trial; or
- relates to whole claim and accepted after relevant period; or
- relates to part of claim, accepted at any time.

Acceptance of part of claim [CPR 36.13 (2)]:
- ends proceedings if C abandons remaining live part of the claim
- if live part not abandoned; Ps proceed to trial and court has discretion re-costs of dead part of claim.

***

CHAPTER 18

Evidence of fact

- Whether case is successful will depend on its facts;
- view Court takes on facts depends on kind and quality of evidence;
- CPR gives Court discretion to exclude admissible evidence in keeping with overriding objective;
- strict rules of evidence do not apply in small claims track.
- Collateral facts - relate to subsidiary matter which can affect whether fact proved, e.g. competence of witness;
- Preliminary facts - relevant to a pre-condition to admissibility of evidence; e.g. credibility; matter must be determined before evidence submitted

Burden of proof - also referred to as legal burden

- obligation imposed on P to prove a fact in issue;
- only one P has burden of proof on any fact;
- P that fails to discharge burden of proof will lose on that issue;
- in Civil cases legal burden may be determined by:
  - agreement between Ps;
  - statute; or
  - common law principles;
- general principle; "he who asserts must prove", applies in 99% of cases;
- where rarely this does not provide answer, Court may ask which P would find it easier to discharge burden of proof.

Standard of proof - "more likely than not":

- in civil cases is balance of probabilities, even where allegation relates to a criminal offence e.g. fraud or assault;
- **standard stays the same, regardless of how serious an allegation is.**

Evidential burden:
- is not a burden of proof;
- just obligation to put forward enough evidence to raise <u>an issue</u> and allow it to go before finder of fact;
- low threshold;
- usually P with legal burden also bears evidential burden on issue;
- are exceptions in criminal cases;
- only exception in civil case is **rebuttable presumption**; producing evidence to contrary is all it takes to rebut presumption in favour of P with legal burden of proof

Presumptions:
- allow fact finder to draw conclusions from other facts;
- <u>presumption of fact</u>; an inference drawn as matter of common sense from facts;
- <u>irrebuttable presumption of law</u>; rule of substantive law; if primary fact proved, presumed facts must be presumed:
  - assumption incapable of being rebutted;
  - e.g.: deeming provision re service of claim form; irrebuttable presumption of due service;
- <u>rebuttable presumptions of law</u>; are true presumptions;
  - purpose to save time in most cases where presumed facts flow from primary fact;
  - presumed facts must be presumed, unless evidence to contrary.

Admissibility of different categories of evidence
- **Opinion;** in general, not admissible, witness must tell Court about facts, not express opinions;
- **Three Exceptions are:**
  <u>1 Opinion of other courts</u>:
- Judgements are form of opinion evidence;
- s11 Civil Evidence Act creates rebuttable presumption that convicted person committed an offence, unless contrary is proved; difficult to rebut this presumption; the conviction must be pleaded in particulars of claim
  [evidence of an acquittal is not admissible in any subsequent trial]
  <u>2 Evidence of witnesses of fact personally perceived</u>:

- witness is allowed to express opinion as way of describing things perceived personally
  3 Expert opinion, see chapter 19 refers

Fact:
- rules require early exchange of evidence of witnesses by exchange of WS; promotes openness and settlement;
- directions to exchange WS usually made on allocation (to fast-track or multitrack) or case management conference;
- WS not normally exchanged in Small Claims track;
- not requirement to disclose WS not intended to call at trial;
- Court can give directions limiting amount and extent of such evidence; identifying who may be called, whose evidence may be, limiting length of WS or limiting issues factual evidence can be directed at;
- normally mutual exchange between Ps ordered; ensures no side revises statements having read other side's as simultaneous;
- normally mutual exchange of WS directed to take place **weeks after disclosure of documents**;
- delay allows witnesses to consider documents disclosed and comment if relevant;
- privilege in WS is waived on disclosure;
- if WS not exchanged as directed, witness may not be called to give oral evidence unless Court gives permission;
- WS should only include admissible evidence and must:
  - include title of proceedings;
  - include information at top about when, by whom and on whose behalf statement made;
  - state whether WS is first or subsequent statement;
  - identify any exhibits;
  - state in opening paragraph why statement has been made;
  - be expressed in first person;
  - make clear what information is not within witnesses own knowledge;
  - any documents referred to must be formally exhibited;

- be verified by statement of truth;
- once verified by statement of truth, false WS may lead to contempt proceedings.

Use of WS at trial:

- WS is means of disclosing what evidence of witness will be;
- WS not evidence itself, unless admitted as hearsay;
- normally evidence at trial given orally on oath;
- where witness called to give evidence, WS stands as evidence in chief, unless court orders otherwise;
  [Court retains discretion to order W give evidence in chief orally]
- where witness gives evidence orally, only with Court's permission can he amplify or give evidence on new matters, re issues arising since statement made:
  - requires good reason;
  - in accordance with overriding objective.
- Where P files WS and fails to attend; evidence in WS not hearsay and automatically relied on by P [Williams v Hinton]
- once called, other P may cross-examine witness on any aspect of disclosed WS;
- where WS not adduced at trial, another P may put disclosed WS in as hearsay, for proceedings in which disclosed;
- WS may only be used more widely if:
  - witness consents in writing;
  - Court gives permission; or
  - WS put in evidence at public hearing.
- **Affidavit**; statement made under oath and witnessed, required for:
  - search orders / freezing injunctions;
  - order requiring occupied to permit another on land
- Affidavits can be used instead of WS but additional cost is not recoverable
- If WS cannot be served in time, then witness summary can be served [CPR 32.9]

Character evidence:
- law lenient about use of bad character evidence in civil cases without jury;
- assumes judges capable of distinguishing evidence relevant to culpability and credibility;
- character evidence can be relevant to:
  - fact in issue;
  - propensity to do what alleged;
  - credibility of witness;
- credibility of people giving evidence is open to attack subject to:
  - Hobbs factors; and
  - Court's general discretion;
- **Hobbs;** questions are acceptable if use would:
  - seriously affect opinion of Court about credibility of witness on matter testified about;
    [if evidence remote in time or nature it may not meet this test]
- So long as evidence **relevant** it will be admitted, unless oppressive or unfair to do so;
- Bad character: argument about whether evidence of should be admitted will turn:
  - *on probative value weighed up against potential prejudicial effect*
- Good character: admissibility depends too on relevance and probative value, bearing in mind we all make mistakes

Witness testimony:
- general rule; all persons are competent (legally capable of giving evidence), and compellable (can be required to give evidence if unwilling to do so voluntarily).
- **Exceptions in criminal cases** about spouses/ civil partners of accused, or D himself, do not apply in civil cases;
- **Exceptions re children and people of unsound mind apply in both criminal and civil cases** but tests differ.

Children: (see also chapter 5)
- **First question**: whether child competent to give sworn evidence.
- Test is R v Hayes; does child understand the:
  - solemnity of occasion; and   [SO]

- - special obligation to tell truth; [SOTT]
- *"is child <u>Hayes appreciative</u>?"*
- if child does not understand oath in Hayes sense consider;

- **Second question; s96 Children's Act 1989 re unsworn evidence**:
  - child's evidence can be heard unsworn if in Court's opinion child understands:
  - duty to tell truth; and has [DTT]
  - sufficient understanding to justify evidence being heard [SU]
  [test stricter than criminal test].
- If child does not pass test for unsworn evidence either, child not competent to give evidence.
  <u>Procedure for assessing child's competence:</u>
- before child gives evidence Court asks child questions;
- enquiries made in open court (except family court);
- children aged 8 to 10 yrs. often able to give sworn evidence;
- for person tendering child as witness to prove child's competence and child judged competent is compellable;
- special arrangements possible to help a child give evidence.
  Special arrangements:
- can be made for any **vulnerable** or **frightened** witness including a child; [VF]
- general rule: evidence given orally in open court;
- Court can control way it receives evidence, allowing witness to use live video link;
- video-conferencing orders also available in all civil cases;
- special measures available in criminal cases used in appropriate civil cases; usually considered at PTR or earlier.
  Persons with mental incapacity:
- not all mental impairment means witness unable to give evidence;
- persons with mental incapacity in civil cases must satisfy Hayes test to be competent;
  [s96 Children's Act does not apply; no provision for people with mental incapacity to give unsworn evidence]

- Court will assess competence before witness evidence is heard;
- expert evidence may be needed about mental condition and potential impact;
- if witness with mental incapacity found competent, he also compellable;
- special measures may be put in place if necessary.

Witness summons

- Where witness competent, almost always compellable;
- Judge is exception; cannot be compelled to give evidence about judicial function;
- compellable witness reluctant to attend may be ordered by witness summons:
    - issued by Court;
    - served at least **7 days before** trial;
    - in civil cases is an administrative process; issue a formality once fee paid and form completed and sealed;
    - permission not required to issue witness summons unless:
    - less than 7 days to trial; or
    - attendance required to give evidence / produce documents at interim hearing or date other than trial;
    - Court can set aside or vary summons; like entering judgement in default in most money claims;
- summons requires one named witness:
    - to attend specified court on specified date and time;
    - in a named case;
    - to give evidence and / or produce specific relevant documents;
    - Court may require earlier production of documents to another P prior to hearing;
    - travelling expenses will be offered or paid;
- witness summons is court order:
    - failure to comply is contempt of court;
    - in CC may be fined, in HC punishable as contempt of court, punishable by fine or imprisonment;

- If no expenses offered or paid to witness in CC, no fine can be imposed;
- separate summons required for each witness.
- Witness summons can help where witness wants to be seen to have been compelled;
- otherwise be cautious about calling reluctant witnesses; their evidence may prove damaging.

Evidence by deposition:
  - if witness cannot attend trial may be possible to obtain order under CPR 34.8; witness gives evidence by deposition;
  - witness gives evidence and examined on oath before Judge or examiner of court.

Adducing evidence at trial - 3 stages

1. **Examination in chief**

- judge may ask questions but is advocates job to question witnesses;
- witness's credibility is relevant fact - it makes his account more or less likely to be true;
- limits on what advocate can do to strengthen quality of evidence being presented as;
  - examination in chief is rare in civil trials; WS often stand as evidence in chief;
  - evidence must come from witness who directly perceived event
  - *[questioning your own witness is to elicit evidence from them, not put words in their mouth];*
- leading questions are prohibited;
- leading question rule is not strictly applied:
  - re introductory or procedural matters;
  - if subject of question not in dispute;

Hostile witness:

- Sometimes witness might get confused or remember something differently;
- nothing advocate can do because of a general rule against contradicting your own witness;

- if witness actively does not wish to tell Court the truth, with Court's permission, witness may be declared hostile;
- allows advocate to:
  - cross-examine own witness;
  - use leading questions; and
  - put to him that he made a **previously inconsistent statement**; typically, earlier WS that not evidence in chief.
- If hostile witness adopts evidence in previous statement, it becomes his evidence on that day;
- if he does not adopt it, previous statement can be proved against him and is admissible as evidence of its truth;
- for Judge to decide which version to believe; current oral evidence, previous statement, or neither.

Rule against previously consistent statements
- Previously consistent statement is made by a witness before trial, consistent with his witness evidence at trial;
- general rule in both criminal and civil cases; such statements not admissible to show consistency with witness's evidence in court.
- Principle is:
  - evidence does not improve through repetition; and
  - witness could manufacture evidence to make story more credible.
- Exceptions to previously consistent statement rule in criminal and civil cases:
  - Statements to rebut an allegation of recent fabrication;
  - memory refreshing documents; and
  - if Court gives permission.

Rebutting allegation of recent fabrication:
- Under cross-examination, witness can point to earlier statements consistent with his evidence in chief;
- may be done in **re-examination** only to extent relevant and necessary to rebut allegation of recent fabrication;
- If allegation is that story has always been untrue, rather than recent fabrication, rule does not apply.

Refreshing memory:

- Witness who has difficulty remembering events giving evidence may refer to a document or written statement to refresh his memory, if conditions are met:
- can be used where witness no longer has any memory of event but can vouch for accuracy of document;
- it is evidence of witness, not the document, that constitutes evidence in the case;
- witnesses can also refresh memory before going in to court from notes and witness statements made by them;
- Judge has discretion in interests of justice to allow witness who has started giving oral evidence to take a break and refresh his memory, provided witness says:
  - he cannot recall detail because of passage of time;
  - statement was made by that witness and closer to the time;
  - statement records his memory at the time;
  - he did not read statement before giving evidence;
  - he wishes to read the evidence before continuing;
  - witness can either withdraw or read statement in the box;
- statement will be removed from witness before he continues to give oral evidence;
- Evidential status of memory refreshing documents: they do not become evidence;
- a cross-examining advocate may inspect any memory refreshing documents without making it evidence;
- he is entitled cross-examine on the document without making it evidence, provided questioning is on parts used by witness to refresh;
- where cross-examination goes beyond parts used in examination in chief, entitles P calling witness to put document in evidence and let Court see it;
- cross examining advocate must weigh up advantages of cross-examining beyond memory refreshing parts against possible disadvantage of entire document being put in evidence.

- Note: the need to refresh memories during oral evidence in chief has reduced as:
  - almost everyone called reads their witness statements to prepare;
  - WS now usually stands as evidence in chief; if evidence not given orally, no scope for refreshing;
  - court has discretion to give P permission to put into evidence a previous consistent statement; allowing P who called witness to admit previous consistent statement instead of using memory refreshing procedures.

2. Cross-examination:
  - leading questions used;
  - cross-examining counsel entitled to discredit witness;
  Two important rules:

1   Rule against rebuttal on collateral issues:
- limits P's ability to contradict witness **in both civil and criminal cases**;
- answers given in cross-examination on collateral matters, such as credibility of witness, which are otherwise irrelevant, may not be contradicted by rebuttal evidence;
- called the **rule of finality of answer** or **rule against rebuttal**;
- prevents advocates getting focused on peripheral issues;
- only applies to matter properly put to witness in cross-examination;
- not always easy to determine which matters collateral:
  - rule precludes rebuttal of evidence re questions going **only** to collateral matters;
  - if questions relate both to witness credibility and a fact in case, the limitation does not apply;

Four Exceptions, where it is possible to adduce evidence to rebut answers on collateral issues:
To prove previous convictions:
- if witness is properly cross-examined about a previous conviction and denies it or doesn't answer, conviction may be proved against him;

- if conviction spent, Judge will consider whether fair to allow questioning of spent conviction.

  To prove witness reputation for untruthfulness:

- witness's credibility maybe impugned by others speaking about his reputation for telling lies. Very rare.

  To prove witnesses bias:

- evidence admissible to contradict any witnesses to show he is prejudiced about outcome of case;
- if witness has vested interest in outcome, fact finding judge should know;
- has to be some basis to be **allegation of bias**.

  To prove physical or mental disability affecting reliability:

- if mental or physical impairment will affect reliability of evidence, judge should know;
- evidence maybe called to prove witness suffers from such disabilities;
- evidence of disability can be used so far as necessary to challenge witness's reliability only.

2   Previously inconsistent statements

- S4 and 5 of CPA 1865 apply to **both civil and criminal cases**;
- provided previously inconsistent statement relevant to subject of proceedings:
    - witness may be cross-examined on previously inconsistent statement; and
    - statement may be adduced to rebut witness's evidence in Court;
- procedure prevents surprises and gives witness chance to prepare to deal with inconsistency; as follows:
    - circumstances of making previous statement are put to witness;
    - he given opportunity to accept truth of that statement;
    - before being contradicted.
- S5 relates to documents only and:
    - witness should be shown statement;
    - asked to read it;
    - asked if he stands by his evidence on oath today – witness may change it, if not;

- advocate may then put document into evidence to show inconsistency.
- In civil cases document will go in for the truth of its contents as no rule against hearsay;
- The advocate must weigh up advantages and possible disadvantages of doing this; other aspects of document may support of other side's case which may not be worth admitting only to show inconsistency

**

CHAPTER 19

Expert Evidence

- General rule: witnesses must give evidence of fact, not opinion;
- inferences to be drawn from facts are matter for judge.
a. 2 main exceptions ;
- **Opinions to convey facts personally perceived:**
  - admissible as evidence of what W perceived; [7]
  - describing "somebody as Caucasian and about 70" is an opinion;
  - used when stating the underlying facts personally perceived would be too onerous.
  b. **Expert evidence**
- Civil cases sometimes require knowledge ordinary people do not have;
- expert opinion is admissible where needed, an exception to general rule;
- expert opinion must be necessary; if matter within experience of most people, expert opinion not admissible;
- Court required to do that which is reasonably required to resolve proceedings;
- CofA guidance says unavailability of experts rarely sufficient grounds to vary directions or trial dates
- expert must be qualified; how expertise acquired (experience or professional qualifications) not important.
- Expert may only give expert opinion on matters within his field of expertise.
  Primary and secondary facts
- Expert witness expresses opinions on facts;
- facts must be proved by admissible evidence, **primary facts;**

---

[7] [s3(2) CEA 1972]

- **secondary facts:** expert may use research papers or books to form his opinion, these need not be admissible but must be available to Court and Ps to examine;
- Expert may express their view on issue but judge will ultimately decide;
- experts assist judge and expert evidence can be rejected if good grounds for doing so.
- Court controls evidence in accordance with overriding objective including expert evidence;
- expert evidence not usually allowed in small claims track;
- directions re expert evidence usually made at case allocation or case management conference;
- **no P may call expert or put expert report in evidence without permission;**
- P must always apply to Court if believes further expert evidence is required;
- when seeking Court's permission, P should provide:
- estimate cost of expert evidence;
- field of expertise;
- issues expert evidence would address;
- expert's name.
- Court does cost benefit analysis to assess if cost justified;
- Court under duty to restrict evidence to that **reasonably required** to resolve proceedings;
- this minimises inappropriate use of experts;
- competing experts may be required in complex claims, most often multitrack;
- in non-complex cases cost of opposing experts unlikely to be justified;
- joint instruction of jointly agreed, **single joint expert** is normal in fast-track cases;
- Ps may have agreed, or Court may make direction on own initiative requiring Ps try to agree a single set of expert instructions;
- if not possible, Ps should disclose to each P the different instructions given;
- expert expresses opinion by report which must:

- be written;
- addressed to Court;
- give details of expert's qualifications;
- instructions given;
- outline who carried out examinations and whether under expert's supervision;
- give any qualification to report;
- summarise conclusions reached;
- where range of opinions, range must be summarised; and
- reasons for expert opinion given;
- be verified by Statement of truth;
- include statement that expert understands duty to court and has complied with it.
- Experts duty summarised in **Ikarian Reefer**, expert:
- evidence should be unbiased, not influenced by litigation;
- should state assumptions;
- should state where an issue is outside their expertise;
- should communicate any change of view without delay;
- plans / measurements / calculations / similar docs must be provided to other Ps when exchanging reports
- where both Ps instruct, both are entitled to a copy of report;
- Ps may ask **written questions** of opposing **experts** [CPR 35.6]:
  - no later than **28 days** after disclosure of report;
  - mutual agreement required if question goes beyond seeking clarification (of what is in report);
  - any answer treated as part of expert's evidence; part of report;
  - a P whose expert does not answer may:
    - o be prevented from relying on report; or
    - o face cost sanctions.
- Process reduces need for expert to attend trial
- At trial:
- in fast track; presumption is single joint expert evidence will be given orally by report:
  - expert will not attend, unless Court orders;
  - expert reports normally represent "evidence in the case", they should not be cross-examined,

- Court has discretion.
- In complex cases Court may allow Ps to have their own expert; more usual on multitrack;
    - same rules about how instructions given, the form of report etc. above apply;
    - <u>Court may direct without prejudice discussions between experts:</u>
        - o experts normally prepare statement for Court setting out issues on which they agree, disagree and why;
        - o Court may specify issues for discussion;
        - o expert agreement does not formally bind Ps but;
        - o will be of weight when Court determines issues;
    - joint experts sit in Court throughout proceedings; and
    - normally give evidence orally;
    - may be cross examined in normal way;
    - if many experts, can take much time, experts going into witness box sequentially;
    - to make process efficient, Court may direct, typically at first CMC, expert evidence be heard **concurrently:**
        - o known as **hot tubbing**;
        - o experts meet to give evidence at same time;
        - o judge asks each expert for views on relevant matters and asks questions;
        - o experts may be asked to comment on evidence of one another;
        - o thereafter Ps may question experts to test or clarify evidence;
        - o Judge may then summarise the different positions

Disclosure of expert evidence pre-trial:
- if Ps jointly instruct a single joint expert, both see report and disclosure happens then;
- in other cases, expert's report is privilege;
- P who is given Court permission and seeks to rely on expert evidence at trial must disclose it before trial;
- privilege must be waived if P wants to use expert evidence at trial;

- rule ensures Ps know case against them and can make decisions accordingly or settle
- Sanctions for non-compliance are severe, if expert report not disclosed before trial may not:
  - use report; or
  - call expert to give evidence orally, unless Court gives permission.
- Where D participated in selection of C's expert, and C chooses not to rely on expert and use another expert, Court may order C to disclose original expert's report to D as price for being allowed to use a new expert;
- known as **Edward Tubb order.**
- Where Ps jointly instruct expert, they see report at outset and disclosure direction not necessary.
- Where directions allow Ps to instruct their own expert they will be directed to exchange expert evidence they propose to call;
- such disclosure normally ordered to be simultaneous but may be sequential, perhaps if it may save costs;
- only evidence a P proposes to adduce at trial needs to be disclosed, subject to Edward Tubb example;
- sometimes a report is disclosed but not relied on at trial;
- then any P to whom report disclosed may bring it in to evidence himself, **but not to impugn it.**

***

CHAPTER 20

Civil Trial, Hearsay and Evidence.

Pre-trial matters can include:

Notices to admit facts: [CPR 32.18]

- P can serve a notice to admit facts on another P; [usually re uncontroversial matters]
- no application to Court required;
- notice served no later than **21 days before trial;** sets out facts to be admitted;
  [facts admitted cease to be in issue at trial]
- if facts not admitted, no sanction in provision but;
- P refusing to admit facts may pay costs of proving same facts, regardless of trial outcome;
- Court required to have regard to conduct of Ps when making order for costs, including if it was reasonable for P to contest an issue; much depends on how reasonable it was not to admit fact.
- Any admission may only be used in proceedings in which notice was served; and only by P who served notice

Notices to prove authenticity of documents: CPR 32.19

- P deemed to admit as authentic documents he inspected on disclosure;
- if authenticity disputed, notice to prove must be sent to disclosing P;
- Notice must be served at later time of:
  - serving WS; or
  - within 7 days of disclosure of documents;
- puts disclosing party on notice that authenticity is in issue.

References to the European Court:

- if domestic court cannot answer a question, a reference to CJEU in Luxembourg may be necessary;
- court usually does this as preliminary issue before trial;
- if references made, domestic trial stayed;
- only judge of Court of Appeal or Supreme Court can refer question.

Human rights issues:

- where court satisfied provision in primary legislation **is not** compatible with Human Rights Convention it may make a declaration of incompatibility;
- details must be set out in statement of case;
- claims for declaration of incompatibility may not be heard below High Court judge;
- if declaration of incompatibility likely, this is a factor in deciding whether to transfer CC case to HC;
- appropriate notice must be given;

Trial arrangements and timetables:

One listed for trial, court makes decisions about:

- whether there are preliminary issues;
- whether trial should not be in public;
- trial timetable; gives structure counsel must operate within; how long to spend on different aspects including:
  - speeches;
  - expert evidence; and
  - questioning, especially cross-examination;
- Ps can express views re timetable in pre-trial checklist, in multitrack cases;
- timetable decisions usually made at pre-trial review, PTR.

Trial bundle:

- all documents likely to be referred to in fast-track or multitrack trial must be in paginated trial bundle;
- C responsible for preparing and filing bundle, **not more than 7 days** and **not less than 3 days** before trial;
- Ps should agree contents as far as possible (rival bundles never lodged);

- an identical bundle should be available to each P, Judge and witnesses;
- unless ruling or order to contrary, all documents in bundle are admissible as evidence of their contents;
- an agreed case summary often helps.

Skeleton arguments (see chapter 23 also):
- used in complex interim applications and compulsory for HC trials;
- often good idea or required by direction in CC too;
- concisely summarises submissions, citing authorities to be relied on;
- filed **2 days before trial** or with trial bundle;
- often good idea to provide short chronology with skeleton

Aspects of Civil Trial running order:
Submission of no case to answer:
- if D making submission of no case to answer, **should first be asked if D wants to call evidence** as potentially compromising to ask single judge sitting alone (norm in civil cases), to rule on merits of claim if evidence incomplete;
- if D calls no evidence, submission of no case to answer will be determined on balance of probabilities and judgement will be entered for P that succeeds on submission;
- if unusually, D not given choice to give evidence, submission determined by reference to whether C has no real prospect of success; if submission fails, D allowed to carry on and call evidence in usual way.

Defence case:
- defence may but usually does not make opening speech;
- calls evidence in same way as C;
- closing speeches where D has called evidence; D's closing speech is before C's;
- closing speech should focus on inferences from evidence and legal points;
- most civil trials before single professional judge; different audience in criminal trials where speech for laypeople.

Judgement:

- judgement often given immediately;
- may be reserved in complex cases;
- once evidence heard, Ps not usually allowed to adduce more evidence but judge may agree, if judgement not yet given, if in keeping with overriding objective;
- once judgement given but before recorded, test is more similar to if case went on to appeal; if CofA would give permission to hear further evidence it is probably sensible for judge to do so;
- when civil trial heard before jury (rare), procedure and conduct of trial more similar to CC.
- Courts have wide discretion re how to proceed.

FastTrack:
- after completion of pre-trial checklist;
- Court gives directions re trial including timetable;
- CPR 28.6.5; provides specimen trial timetable and acts as templates to fast-track trials;
- maximum of **five hours** presumes trial judge has pre-read papers.

On multitrack :
- after completion of pre-trial checklist or holding of pre-trial review;
- Court sets timetable for trial;
- Ps notified of trial timetable and date for trial;
- timeline of civil trial normally;
    - Cs opening speech, D opening speech,
    - [no examination in chief]
    - Cross-examination of C's witnesses by D, Re-examination by C, if any
    - Cross-examination of D's witnesses by C, Re-examination by D if any
    - Ds submissions, Cs submissions
- Judgement, Costs and consequential orders

Calling and examining witnesses - different from Criminal trials [CPR 32.2- CPR 32.13]:
- normal method for producing evidence is calling a witness;
- traditionally in civil trials; following service of WS, witness:
    - called;
    - sworn or affirmed;

- verifies statement theirs;

[WS stands as evidence in chief, unless court orders otherwise]

- P not calling witness then cross-examines using leading questions;
- witness then re-examined only re matters raised in cross-examination;
- Court may allow witness to give evidence via video link [CPR 32.3];
- if P wishes to adduce evidence such as:
- plans;
- photographs;
- models;
- and evidence not in or exhibited in WS; P must give notice of evidence at time of serving WS [8]

Hearsay in civil proceedings

- Hearsay is admissible in civil proceedings[9], can be defined as;
  *"An assertion not made by a person giving evidence in court but which is nevertheless
  relied upon to establish the truth of what was asserted";*

  or
  a statement
  made by a person
  not made in oral evidence in court
  tendered as evidence of matters stated

- if tribunal of fact asked to believe what said in statement is true, assertion is hearsay;
- if tribunal fact is asked to believe statement is relevant for another purpose, it is not hearsay.

---

[8] [CPR 33.6]

[9] s1(1) Civil Evidence Act 1995

- Evidence not excluded in civil trials on grounds of being hearsay except where:
    - witness not competent when statement made; or
    - statement is opinion.
- Only issue for judge considering hearsay is **what weight** to give it according to factors including:
- reliability of evidence;
    - how easy it would have been to call witness to give direct evidence;
    - how close in time statement made to events described;
    - whether may be ulterior motive to keep witness away;
    - whether involves multiple hearsay;
    - extent to which P relying on hearsay complied with notice rules;
- important to know whether evidence is hearsay because need to give advance notice of intention to adduce it:

    How notice given of intention to adduce hearsay; depends on its form:
- if hearsay within evidence of witness being called, beyond exchange of WS, nothing further done;
- where WS of person not being called, P intending adduce must "inform" (no formal notice) Ps of that intention when exchanging WS, and explain why witness not called
  [with Court's permission, other P may require witness to attend to be cross examined on statement];
- if hearsay takes other form, for example an invoice not exhibited in WS, P wanting to adduce it must serve formal notice on other P clearly identifying hearsay, stating intention to adduce and giving reasons for not calling maker of statement. **Notice served no later than the time for exchange of WS**.
- Failure to comply with hearsay notice rules does not render hearsay inadmissible but can effect:
    - weight given to it; or
    - result in adverse costs order.

- For Court to decide what evidence it wants to hear, on which issues and in what form.
- Court always has power to exclude admissible evidence if it would be in keeping with overwriting objective

Three types of Hearsay statements:

	Type of hearsay to be given	Notice Procedure Required
1	Hearsay given orally	give noticed by serving WS [as WS normally exchanged, requires no additional procedural step]
2	Hearsay evidence in WS but witness not available	give notice by serving WS informally inform P that witness will not attend trial give reasons for absence
3	All other cases	serve formal notice at time serves WS, identify hearsay say P intends to rely on hearsay

Options available to P served with hearsay notice are:
- request particulars of evidence;
- make submission aimed at reducing weight of hearsay including;
- whether original statement made at same time as another matter
- motive of statement maker
- where witness not available; may additionally:
  - apply to cross examine witness with **permission to amplify*** (only if no good reason for absence);
  - call evidence to attack credibility (**notice to attack needed**);
  - application and notice must be made **within 14 days of service of hearsay notice.**

Convictions as evidence in civil proceedings:
- evidence of previous and current convictions may be used in civil proceedings where relevant;
- person presumed to have committed offence unless proved otherwise[10];
- any evidence of conviction is admissible and certified documents presumed true.

Summary:
- civil approach to witness handling differs from criminal approach;
- WS usually stands as witnesses evidence in chief subject to **permission to amplify*;**
- failure to comply with hearsay rule does not automatically render hearsay inadmissible;
- Court retains wide discretion.

***

---

[10] s11 Civil Evidence Act 1968

CHAPTER 21

Judgements, orders and enforcement

*NB: You might be feeling exhausted but keep going, you can do this.
You're nearly there.
Don't give up at enforcement, it does come up in exams...*

- After interim application, Court may make <u>an order</u>;
- after trial, Court may make <u>final judgement</u>;
- after final judgement pronounced, final judgement must be drawn up;
- general rule; Court responsible for drawing up judgement[11]:
    - Court may give order or permission for a P to write up judgement;
    - Courts may dispense with needs to draw up;
    - in QBD, inc Commercial Court (not Admiralty), general rule reversed; unless Court orders otherwise, judgement must be drawn up by Ps;
- **power to check;** court may still direct that:
    - judgement or order drawn up by P is checked by Court before sealed; or
    - before judgement or order drawn up by Court, Ps must file an agreed statement of terms.
- a P required to draw up has **7 days to file** relevant documents;
- failing that, any other P may draw up and file;
- Court will serve a copy on each P;
- most judgements and orders must state name and judicial title of person who made it;
- unless Court specifies otherwise, **judgement takes effect from date given**, not date drawn up and served;

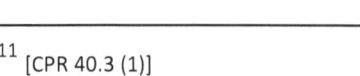

---

[11] [CPR 40.3 (1)]

- unless Court specifies otherwise, interest runs from date judgement given;
- like interim injunctions, final injunctions must contain **penal notice;** warning of consequences of breach, and are:
- not enforceable until respondent made aware of order, usually by being personally served or;
- being in court to hear it
  [because until P knows he is ordered to do something he cannot be expected to comply];
- judgement for **payment of money including costs must be complied with within 14 days of order,** unless Court or CPR specifies otherwise, or Court stays proceedings;
- where order imposes time limit for act, deadline for compliance must be clear, including date and time [12]
  - consequences for failure to act in time may be specified in order:
  - very specific language needed; called **"unless order",** for example
  "Unless C/D serves list of documents by ... date his claim/ defence will be struck out and Judgement entered for D/C"
  - If P1 fails to comply with unless order, P2 may:
- obtain judgement with costs; by
- filing request for judgement using CPR 23 application
- defaulting P1 - can apply to set judgement aside within **14 days** of judgement.

Judgements on both claim and counterclaim: [13]

- Where court gives judgement:
  - for C on claim; and
  - against C, on counter claim (at same time);
  - Court may order payment of balance only.

---

[12] PD 40B 147.

[13] CPR 40.13

At any time, court can correct error in judgment or order:[14]
- application notice is informal and should set out error and correction needed;
- P may apply for correction without notice;
- court may direct notice be given;
- if application opposed, should be hearing before a judge.

Many judgements or orders are made by consent:[15]
- true consent order is record of contractual agreement between Ps only varied on grounds rendering contract void or voidable, such as fraud or misrepresentation;
- Ps may agree terms of judgement or order **and Court will record that:**
  - order / judgement is by consent and
  - signed by Ps
- Court may generally give a judgement agreeable to all Ps; they may have suggested its terms, yet this is not a true consent order, in contractual sense, and enforcement is like any other court order or judgement.

Tomlin orders:
- special kind of consent order used where;
  - complex terms agreed; or
  - terms go beyond original issues or exceed Court's jurisdiction;
- has effect of staying claim, except as necessary for purpose of implementing obligations in schedule
- court officer must enter and seal Tomlin Order if satisfied;
  - no P is litigant in person
  - court approval is not required, by CPR or statute;
- 2 parts to Tomlin Order:
- The Order; issues court has jurisdiction over:
- main issues;

---

[14] [CPR 40.12]

[15] **[CPR 40.6]:**

- costs;
- confirms proceedings stayed except for purposes of
1. carrying out terms of schedule, and
2. liberty to apply to court to carry terms into effect
  Schedule attached; not part of order:
- enforced through different mechanism,
- binding contract between Ps but not directly enforced (schedule contains issues outside court jurisdiction)
  Enforcing terms of schedule if breached is 2 stage process:
- claim must be restored; and
- order sought, to compel compliance with term (using 'at liberty to apply' clause)
  (If 2nd order breached, enforcement is via usual methods.)
- 2 categories of case where may set aside or vary TO:
- date of order, was error of fact;
- material or unforeseen change in circumstances after order, undermine / invalidate basis of order.
- A non-party to judgement or order directly affected by it may apply to court to have it varied or set aside **CPR 40.9**

Enforcement of judgements and orders:
- not everyone abides by court orders;
- if money judgement made against someone with no money or assets, may be little a P can do;
- if person has money but will not pay, Court has powers to enforce compliance;
- choice of enforcement method decided according to circumstances *[only money judgements will be referred to in this book].*

Seizure and sale of goods:
- CC has warrants of control;
- HC writs of control;
- CC cannot issue warrant for judgements exceeding £5000; matter must be transferred to HC;
- issuing writ or warrant of control is administrative process;

- but if 6 years has elapsed since judgements, permission to enforce required.
- Once order received, enforcement officer of Court will:
- visit judgement debtor's premises;
- not force entry, unless reasonable force sanctioned by Court order;
- assert control over named goods;
- if payment of judgement debt not made within minimum period of notice, goods can be sold to satisfy debt;
- some goods exempt: domestic necessities, tools of debtor's trade, goods belong to someone else, e.g. hire purchase goods.

Charging orders:
- may be possible to get charge against property;
- person must have equity;
- procedure involves two stages:
- **getting charging order**, an interim order- may prove incentive enough for judgement debtor to pay;
- hearing **converting charge into cash;** giving interested Ps opportunity to make submissions re why interim order should not now be made final;
- where value of charge exceeds £350,000, only HC can order sale.

Third party debt orders:
- useful if someone owes money to judgement debtor;
- order requires person owing money to judgement debtor to pay it to judgement creditor directly;
- not possible if account is held jointly with an innocent other as account cannot be enforced against;
- like a charging order, third-party debt order as a two stage procedure.

Attachment of earnings:
- may be only option where judgement debtor has salary but no assets;
- order directs employer to deduct and pay to Court named amount from employee's salary;
- orders can only be made in CC, following order for payment by instalments which has fallen into arrear;

Judgmt order - Taxes effect frm th day it
is given or made (or cnt speil

Intemt begin to run - Date that judgmt's giu
(enlen cout rule or PD
says othrwise).

- amount deducted is limited by a formula to ensure judgement debtor has enough to live on.

Committal proceedings: apply only to non-money judgements:
- non money judgements such as injunctions enforced differently;
- failure to comply can amount to contempt of court;
- requires intervention of Court via **committal order;**
- proceedings for contempt are punitive, two main punishments are:
  1. imprisonment for up to 2 years which can be suspended and/or fine limited to £2500 in CC; or
  2. sequestration of assets.
- These are serious matters therefore to establish contempt;
- breach must be shown to be **intentional** and
- standard of proof is **criminal standard**; beyond reasonable doubt and
- must show judgement or **order contained a penal notice** warning of consequences of breach and
- was **served personally on P**, unless Court orders otherwise
- Procedurally, committal order applied for using <u>normal Part 23 procedure</u>, or Part 8 if no proceedings underway
- application notice must:
- set out grounds; and
- unusually, written evidence in support must be by **affidavits**
- hearing is before Circuit or HC judge;
- committal proceedings can also be used to enforce a breach of an undertaking given to Court by party as undertakings are sometimes given in lieu of order being made

Consent orders -
Court office cannot enter and seal
agreed judgment or order if -
- none of the parties are litigant in person

This can -
- Payment of an amount of money (damages
or the value of goods to be decided by the
court)
- delivery up of goods,

Party against whom a judgment has been given may apply to Court for –

– A stay of execution, or

– other relief

on the ground of matters which have occurred

Since the date of judgment

Transfer of proceedings may be needed for enforcement, in summary:

From ⇒ To	Must be transferred if JC seeks
CC ⇒ HC	➡execution against goods worth more than £5000 or ➡enforcement of charging order by sale exceeding £350k
HC ⇒ CC	against goods or judgement of < £600 charging order where judgement debt £5000 or less attachment of earnings order
CC ⇒ CC in JD'S district	info from a JD or TP debt in money order claim charging order attachment of earnings order

Where a judgement or an order is to be drawn up by ~~the court~~ a party*** –

– He must file it no later than 7 days after the date on which the court ordered

If he fails to do so, any other party may draw it up and file it

CHAPTER 22

Costs

- What Court orders for costs depends on many factors, including conduct of litigants.
- Idea is to make litigation unattractive; choice of last resort.
- General rule: loser pays winners costs ("costs follow the event");
- sometimes called "cost shifting", winner's obligation to pay his legal costs shifts to loser.

Court's powers re misconduct:
- to fall within rule, P or legal representative in summary or detailed costs assessment must:
  - fail to comply with rule, PD or order or
  - conduct of P or legal rep before or during assessment proceedings was unreasonable or improper;
- Court may disallow all or part of costs; or
- order P or legal rep to pay costs they caused another P to incur.
- If order made and P absent, legal rep obliged to notify P within **7 days** of legal rep being notified

General approach to costs:
- At end of hearing Court has to decide :
- whether costs order made;
- basis of assessment (indemnity or standard); [BIS]
- method of assessment (summary or detailed);
- amount of costs;
- when payable.
- Court's costs discretion is **VERY broad**[16],
- Costs within courts discretion are costs:
  - of proceedings; or
  - incidental to proceedings.

---

[16] **CPR 44.2**

- Deciding costs order, court has regard to all the circumstances including parties conduct:[17]
  - before and during proceedings;
  - compliance with pre-action protocols or PD-PAC;
  - if was reasonable to raise / pursue / contest an issue;
  - the way P pursued / defended case, an allegation or issue;
  - if successful C exaggerated claim;
  - if P succeed on part of case, even if didn't win;
  - admissible **non-**Part 36 offers made.

Interim cost orders [PD 44 (4.2)]

- Are many different interim applications, at end of which an order for costs follows called **interim cost order.**
- Costs re interim applications are at Court's discretion and usually favour successful P.
- Order Judge makes depends on situation, possible interim cost orders include:
  - costs in the case: winner at trial wins cost of interim application;
  - C or D's costs in the case, is more favourable: if named P wins at trial he wins costs of interim application too, if he loses he only pays his own costs of that application;
  - each P to pay its own costs;
  - no order as to costs: each P pays its own costs
- General rule; if order makes no reference to costs; non payable [CPR 44.10 (1)]

Type of Interim Costs order	Effect
Costs / costs in any event	Successful P entitled to costs
Costs in the case / application	Successful P **in trial** entitled to costs (for proceedings order relates to)

---

[17] **44.2 (6)**

Costs reserved	Decision deferred. If no later order, costs in the case applies.
C or D's costs in the case / application	If named P wins trial he wins costs of that interim application, if he loses he only pays his own cost of that application
Costs thrown away	Where judgement / order **set aside**, winner receives costs incurred as consequence
Costs of and caused by	Following application by P1 to **amend statement of case**, P1 bears costs of P2 preparing / attending application and costs of amendment
Cost here and below	Successful P entitled to costs for application and costs for proceedings in lower courts

Displacement of general rule - "Different orders" can include;
- successful party pays own costs + losers costs (rare);
- More commonly a hybrid e.g.: issue-based / percentage based / date specific order / order re distinct parts of proceedings
- if winner failed on discrete issue, may deprive costs re issue and/or order to pay losers costs re it (Johnsey Estates)

Advocate's responsibility to seek appropriate order for costs
Four possible basis for assessment:
1. Costs agreed by Ps
2. Costs fixed;
- set amount fixed by reference to value of case; keep lawyers' fees down and
- used for early disposal of simple cases, unless Court orders otherwise
- Small claims track cases where no lawyers' fees recoverable but fixed amounts for Court costs and expenses recoverable, subject to reasonable behaviour;
  [this is not a no costs rule as only lawyer's costs are irrecoverable]

- Brief fees (advocates fees) for fast-track are fixed by reference to value of judgement, or amount on claim form if D wins. Fixed rate covers advocate's fee only, other costs are not fixed.
- Relevant amounts are subjects to discretion of Court and may be reduced if behaviour warrants.

3. Costs Summarily assessed; quantified on the day on approximate basis:

- determined immediately at end of hearing - unless good reason not to;
- winners ask for costs to be assessed using schedule of costs fixed **24 hours** before interim hearing and **2 days before fast-track trial**;
- Court works through statement of costs served;
- Other side may dispute some figures;
- summary assessment is used for:
  - interim hearings of less than 1 day;
  - appeals of less than 1 day;
  - unreasonable behaviour assessments in small claims cases;
  - most fast-track final cost orders, the brief fees being fixed;
  - summary assessment is not appropriate in legal aid cases or cases involving children;
- costs generally **payable within 14 days** of order; Court retains discretion.

4. Detailed assessment:

- complex procedure for:
  - long interim applications;
  - multitrack cases that run into **multiple days;**
  - complex cases;
- Detailed assessment mandatory if:
  - receiving P has legal aid / publicly funded;
  - money claimed for benefit of child or protected P;
- assessment by **a costs judge;** DJ in CC or judges in senior court costs office in HC;
- assessment **hearing within 3 months of judgement**;
- in deciding what order to make, Court has regards to all the circumstances including:
  - amounts involved;

- conduct of P in way pursued or defended case;
- whether P partially or fully successful;
- importance of matter to Ps;
- complexity or novelty of question;
- skill, effort, specialised knowledge and responsibility required;
- time spent;
- place where and circumstances in which work done
- offers in settlement made.

- Approach takes into account all circumstances so award is case sensitive, possibilities include Court ordering:
- percentage of another P's costs;
- stated amount of another P's costs;
- costs from or until specified date;
- costs incurred before proceedings began;
- costs relating to particular steps in proceedings;
- interest on costs from or until a certain date;
- issue based costs get complicated and simpler alternatives including percentage awards are now more common.
- **Payment on account of costs:** In cases subject to detailed assessment, Court will order P to pay reasonable sum on account unless good reason not to do so
  [receiving P thus receives part payment upfront during delay awaiting detailed assessment].
- P must comply with **order** for costs within 14 days of: [18]
  - date of judgement or order, if summarily assessed;
  - date of certificate stating amount, if subject to detailed assessment, or
  - or other date specified by court

Basis of Assessment [19]

- Standard basis; any doubt resolved in favour of payer; keeping their expense to a minimum

---

[18] CPR 44.7

[19] CPR 44.3

- Indemnity basis; any doubt resolved in favour of payee (who thus gets more)
- Reasonable: both basis only allow such costs as reasonable in **amount** and reasonably **incurred**
- Standard basis has further requirements of proportionality
- disproportionate costs may be disallowed even if reasonably incurred

[key question is: did value and complexity of case justify expense?]

Standard basis	Indemnity basis
Reasonably and **proportionately** incurred [i]	Reasonably incurred
Reasonable and **proportionate** in amount [a]	Reasonable in amount
If in doubt resolve in favour of payer	If in doubt resolve in favour of receiving P

Summary of factors re basis

Funding litigation

- **In general, Ps' method of funding litigation does not affect costs.** Six options are:
- legal aid; rarely available;
- trade union or other third-party funding;
- BTE - before the event insurance; typically, home or motor insurance;
- ATE - after the event insurance; taken out after need arises often to cover adverse costs, can be expensive;
- CFA - conditional fee agreements; a no win no fee:
  - if client loses, he pays nothing;
  - if client wins, solicitors charge usual rate plus pre-arranged uplift as **success fee;**
  - additional ATE insurance protects against other side's costs;
  - now success fee and ATE insurance fee are not recoverable from loser, as result;

- **DBA - damages based agreements**; new variant available in all civil claims: [dba]
  - client pays nothing whilst litigation running;
  - if client loses, he pays nothing;
  - if he wins, client agrees to pay **out of damages** recovered, including counsel's fees, typically a percentage:
    - not exceeding 50% of sums recovered in non PI claims;
    - not exceeding 25% of PSLA and past pecuniary loss, taking nothing from future pecuniary loss;
    - DBA must be in writing, setting out terms clearly.

Special costs

- **Court can make Bullock or Sanderson order where C succeeds against only some Ds**
- When choosing, court looks at all facts.
- Where C sues two Ds and succeeds against D1 but not against D2; costs follow the event would mean C recovers costs from D1 and C pays costs to successful D2.
- Where it was reasonable to proceed against both D's, Court has discretion to make 2 other orders:
  1. Bullock order; *B/BAD*
- C pays D1 costs
- D2 pays C's costs plus + **reimburses** C for D1's costs, once paid
  2. Sanderson Order. *(S simpler)*
- D2 ordered to pay C's costs and D1's costs **directly,** not rooted via C.
- C has no liability to pay D1 costs.
- Order appropriate if C is insolvent or publicly funded as greater certainty money of reaching winning D.

Claim and counterclaim:

- Where counterclaim amounts to total setoff, D1 and being successful and costs will be follow the event;
- Where set off less than C's claim, D should make Part 36 offer for balance to protect himself on costs because (unless set-off fails), C can never beat the offer;

- Where both claim and counterclaim succeed or fail, traditionally there should be two judgements and two separate orders as to costs, known as the rule in "Medway oil"

Pro bono costs:
- pro bono representation is undertaken free;
- Court can order losing P to make payment to prescribed charity; the Access to Justice Foundation;
- such order possible in all courts;
- discretion is exercised:
    - loser pays costs he otherwise liable to pay but to charity directly;
    - fixed costs may be awarded, otherwise court will assess on summary or detailed basis;
    - summary assessment generally better; saves money and gets payment to charity quickly.

***

CHAPTER 23

Civil **Appeals CPR 52.3**

Important to know:
- where an appeal lies;
- whether permission required to appeal;
- whether grounds must be shown; or
- if appeal is dealt with by rehearing.

General Rule:
- appeal lies to next judge up in Court hierarchy (not necessarily next court up) so that;
- District judge appeal goes to Circuit Judge, Circuit Judge appeal goes to High Court Judge, etc.
     District Judge ⇒ *Circuit judge* ⇒ *High Court Judge* ⇒...
- There are exceptions;
- In 1st appeal from CC or Master in HC, must distinguish interim and final decision, and if final, note track case on as;
- 1st appeal from final decision of District or Circuit judge or High Court Master, in Part 7 multitrack or specialist claim goes direct Court of Appeal
- **A decision is final:**
    - if it determines entire proceedings; or
    - is decision on a preliminary matter with the same effect, e.g.; question of whether action is time barred.
- **Following are not final** decisions (although they may feel like it), but classic interim remedies:
- order to strike out;
- summary judgement;
- most case management decisions.
- Occasionally; appeals miss an intermediate tier on their way from High Court so:

- decision of Master could go straight to ⇒ Court of Appeal (skipping High Court judge tier);
- decision of High Court Judge could go straight to ⇒ Supreme Court (skipping Court of Appeal tier);
- happens rarely, only when an appeal raises **significant point of principle or practice**;
  o as happened in Mitchell v News Group Newspapers.

Leave to appeal always required:
- Generally, permission to appeal always required unless individual appealing's liberty is at stake, which is rare;
- permission sought by asking Court below first;
- if lower Court refuses, permission may be sought from appeal court.
- **Application made:**
  - at hearing to be appealed; or
  - to appeal court in appeal notice.

To appeal appellant must:
- **within 21 days** of decision, **file an appeal notice** setting out;
- grounds on which judgement is wrong;
- if permission to appeal is required, even if made orally, request to appeal must be repeated in appeal notice;
- appeal notice must be **served on other P within 7 days of being filed**;
- time limits varied only by permission of appeal Court but agreement of A and R to extension not sufficient;
- appeal court can give permission to appeal from paperwork alone;
- if permission refused, applicant can then ask that matter be reconsidered at an oral hearing;
- Court has discretion to refuse.
- **First and second appeals:**
- second appeals always go to Court of Appeal;
- easier to get permission for 1st appeal, test:
- test is: **real prospect of success** or
- **some other compelling reason**;
  [same test as applied in summary judgement]
- 2nd appeal test is more stringent:

- permission must be sought from Court of Appeal:
- test is: raises an **important point of law or principal** or **some other compelling reason**.
- Rspondent in any appeal **may** file and serve respondents' notice;
  - **must** do so if respondent is seeking permission to appeal; or
  - wishes superior court to uphold the lower court decision for different reasons
    - *then the different reasons must be set out.*
- R notice must be **filed** with appeal Court in time directed by lower Court, if no direction should file within **14 days** from:
- R being served with A's notice;
- being notified appeal Court has given A permission to appeal;
- date R notified A's application to appeal and the appeal itself will be heard together.
- R's notice should be **served** as soon as practicable and not more than **7 days** after filing with court

Skeleton arguments:
- must be provided in appeals to Court of Appeal; and
- may be provided where skeleton would help court in way not obvious from other documents;
- **skeleton** should contain:
  - summary of submissions;
  - no more than 25 pages;
  - give reason if using more than 1 authority per point of law;
  [can be cost consequences for non-compliance]
Review of decision - not rehearing:
- most appeals involve reviewing decision of Court below, not rehearing;
- Judges have much discretion and appeals are lost or won on question of:
- whether decision plainly wrong; or
- otherwise unjust, because of some procedural or other irregularity;
- for this reason, appellate Court will not review evidence not put before lower Courts;

- Fresh evidence only rarely permitted on appeal, for example; where credible evidence not available at trial could have been important; Ladd v Marshall

Generally, in Summary:
- first appeal generally goes to next tier of judge;
- some appeals fast-tracked to Court of Appeal;
- if first appeal from CC or High Court Master ask:
  - is decision final;
  - if decision interim; as most case management decisions are, appeal goes to next court rung up;
  - if decision final, look to see what track cases on;
- if case on multitrack, appeal goes to ⇒ Court of Appeal
- if not, will go to the next court rung up, as usual
- Second appeals always go to ⇒ Court of Appeal
  Permission not needed where appeal against:
  - committal order;
  - refusal to grant habeas corpus (writ bringing person before court);
  - secure accommodation order.

Routes of appeal; generally, to next level judge except; part 7 claim in final proceedings on multitrack, appeal to CofA

Stay pending appeal, CPR 52.7:
- appeal does not stay any order, unless lower or appeal court orders otherwise;
- P winning in lower courts can enforce judgement or order;
- if loser applies for stay, court will consider whether risk of injustice if stay granted.

Appeal court has all the powers of lower Court and can:
- affirm, set aside, vary order or judgement;
- refer matter back to lower court;
- order new trial or new hearing, but not where claim tried by jury;
- make order for payment of interest;
- order costs.

If appeal court:
- refuses application for permission to appeal;
- strikes out A's notice; or
- dismisses appeal;
- and considers notice or appeal **totally without merit** appeal court order **must record this** and
    - consider civil restraint order.

Appeal may succeed on grounds decision was **wrong in** law / fact / exercise of discretion / **unjust** because of serious procedural or other irregularities.

***

CHAPTER 24

Revision tips and CPR to learn by heart.

There is so much to learn for civil that if you can't manage it all, at times you may have to make a judgement call. The following is a list of CPR rules etc. which you should try to learn. You may wish to add to it. Where it may not be necessary to know statute verbatim, the text is shown in pale grey. This has been summarised to help with revision and does not mirror all subsection numbers, so please make sure that you are happy with the summaries and refine them to make them your own. The process should help with memorisation. Do compare them with the original text of the CPR. The BSB syllabus evolves over time so time please check that this list reconciles with your very latest syllabus.

CPR

***

3.4—Power to strike out case – see chapter 12
- ref to statement of case [SofC] includes ref to part of a SofC.
- court may strike out SofC if appears to court it:
• discloses no reasonable grounds for bringing / defending claim;
• is an abuse of process or otherwise likely to obstruct just disposal of proceedings; or
• has been failure to comply with rule, PD or court order.

3.9—Relief from sanctions– see chapter 12
• On application for relief from sanction imposed for failure to comply with rule, PD or court order, court will consider all circumstances, to enable it to deal justly with application, including need—
• for litigation to be conducted efficiently and at proportionate cost; and
• to enforce compliance with rules, PD and orders.
➡ Application for relief must be supported by evidence.

***

***

12.3—To obtain Judgement in default– see chapter 11

- C may obtain judgment in default only if—
- D has not filed acknowledgment of service or defence to claim (or any part of claim); and
- relevant time has expired.

- Judgment in default ...may be obtained —
➡ where acknowledgment of service filed but defence not filed;
➡ in counterclaim made under r20.4, where defence not filed, and, in either case, time limit has expired.
- C may not obtain default judgment where—
• D has applied—
- to have C's SofC struck out, rule 3.4; or
- for summary judgment, under Part 24, and application has not been disposed of;
• D has satisfied whole claim (including costs) on which C seeking judgment;
- C is seeking judgment on claim for money; and
- D has filed or served on D admission of liability to pay all of the money claimed with request for time to pay;
• ...

13.2 Court must set aside judgment entered under Part 12...
if judgment wrongly entered because—
- any conditions in r12.3(1) and 12.3(3) not satisfied;
- any conditions in r12.3(2) and 12.3(3) not satisfied; or
- whole claim was satisfied before judgment entered.

13.3 Court may set aside or vary judgment entered under Part 12 ....
• In any other case, court may set aside or vary judgment if—
- D has real prospect of successfully defending claim; or
- some other good reason why—
• judgment should be set aside or varied; or
• D should be allowed to defend it.
• court will consider whether person seeking to set aside judgment made application promptly.
(Rule 3.1(3): court may attach conditions when makes order.)

***

17.1—Amendments to statements of case – see chapter 9

- P may amend statement of case at any time before served on other P.
- Where served, P may amend only with—
∗ written consent of all Ps; or
∗ permission of court.
- If statement of case served, application to amend by removing, adding or substituting P must be made per rule 19.4.
  (Part 22: amendments to statement of case are verified by statement of truth, unless court orders otherwise.)

17.4—Amendments to statements of case after end of limitation period

- where P applies to amend statement of case; and limitation has expired ......
- court may allow amendment to add or substitute new claim, only if new claim arises out of same facts or substantially same facts as claim already claimed.
- court may allow amendment to correct mistake re name of P, only where mistake genuine, not one causing reasonable doubt re identity of P.
- court may allow amendment to alter capacity in which P claims if new capacity is one P had when proceedings started or has since acquired.

***

18.1—Obtaining further info– see chapter 10

- court may at any time order party to—
∗ clarify matter in dispute in proceedings; or
∗ give additional info re any such matter,
  whether or not matter referred to in statement of case.
- ...
- Where court makes order under (1), P against whom made must—
- file response; and
- serve it on other Ps,
  within time specified by court.

Part 22 requires response be verified by statement of truth.

***

19.2—Rules re Changes of Ps– see chapter 8

- rule applies where P is to be added or substituted except where case falls within rule 19.5 (special provisions after end of relevant limitation period).
- court may order P to be added as new P if—
➡ desirable so court can resolve all matters in dispute; or
➡ is issue involving new P and existing P connected to matters in dispute in proceedings, and is desirable to add new P to resolve issue.
- court may order any person to cease being P if not desirable for person to be P to proceedings.
- court may order new P to be substituted for existing one if—
＊ existing P's interest or liability pass to new P; and
＊ desirable to substitute new P so court can resolve matters in dispute in proceedings.

19.5—Adding or substituting Ps after end of limitation period

1. …
- court may add or substitute P only if—
- relevant limitation period was current when proceedings started; and
- addition or substitution is necessary.
- addition or substitution of P is necessary only if court satisfied—
- new P to be substituted for P, named in claim form in mistake for new P; or
- claim cannot properly be carried on by or against original P unless new P added or substituted as C or D; or
- original P died or had bankruptcy order against him and his interest or liability passed to new P.

- In addition, in claim for PI court may add or substitute P where it directs that—
-
- s 11 (special time limit for claims for personal injuries); or

- s 12 (special time limit for claims under fatal accidents legislation), of the Limitation Act 1980 shall not apply to claim by or against new P; or
- the issue of whether those sections apply is to be determined at trial.

***

24.2 Grounds for summary judgment– see chapter 11
court may give summary judgment against C or D on whole claim or 1 issue if—
- it considers —
- C has no real prospect of success; or
- D has no real prospect of successfully defending; **and**
- no other compelling reason why case or issue should be disposed of at trial.
(Rule 3.4 makes provision for court to strike out statement of case or part statement of case if discloses no reasonable grounds for bringing or defending claim.)

***

25.7—Conditions for Interim payments– see chapter 15
- court may only make order for interim payment where any of following satisfied—
- D admitted liability to pay damages or other sum of money to C;
- C obtained judgment against D for damages to be assessed or for money (not costs) to be assessed
- it is satisfied, if claim went to trial C, would obtain judgment for substantial sum of money (other than costs) against D whether or not D is only D or one of a number of Ds to claim;
- the following conditions are satisfied—
- the C is seeking an order for possession of land; and
- court is satisfied if case went to trial, D would be held liable (even if claim for possession fails) to pay C sum of money for D's occupation and use of land while claim for possession was pending; or

- in a claim in which there are two or more D and the order is sought against any one or more Ds, following conditions satisfied—
- court is satisfied if claim went to trial, C would obtain judgment for substantial amount of money (other than costs) against at least one Ds (but court cannot determine which); and
- all Ds are either—
- insured re the claim;
- a D whose liability will be met by insurer under section 151 of Road Traffic Act 1988 or Motor Insurers Bureau Agreement, or Motor Insurers Bureau where it is acting itself; or
- a D that is a public body.
- -
- -
- court must not order interim payment more than reasonable proportion of likely final judgment.
- court must take into account—
- contributory negligence; and
- set-off or counterclaim.

***

25.13—Conditions for security for costs– see chapter 15
- court may make order for security for costs if—
- satisfied, having regard to all circumstances, it is just to do so; and
- ..
- conditions are—
- C is—
1. resident out of jurisdiction; but
2. not resident in a Brussels Contracting State, a State bound by the Lugano Convention, a State bound by the 2005 Hague Convention or a Regulation State, as defined in section 1(3) of the Civil Jurisdiction and Judgments Act 1982;
- [omitted]
- **C is Co or other body** (in or out GB) and reason to believe unable to pay D's costs if ordered;
- …

25. 13. 13 **Particular discretionary factors where condition (c) relied on**

Court has discretion under r.25.13 whether to order security for costs having regard to all circs of case. Among circs court might take into account (per(Sir Lindsay Parkinson & Co v Triplan Ltd [1973] Q.B. 609, CA, per Lord Denning M.R.) include:

- C's claim bona fide not sham;
- C has reasonably good prospect of success;
- admission by Ds that money is due;
- substantial payment into court or an "open offer" of a substantial amount;
- application for security used oppressively, e.g. to stifle genuine claim;
- C's want of means is result of conduct by D; e.g. delay in payment;
- application for security is made at late stage of proceedings.

***

American Cyanamid Co Note

- principles based on "great object" of court hearing application for interlocutory injunction;
  "abstain from expressing opinion on merits of case until hearing".
- objective to prevent court from bogged down with issues, not suitable for determination in interim hearing,
- where trial date likely to be long way off.
- principles crude case management rules designed to reduce cost and delay
- avoid case being tried twice, whilst
- preserving status quo so far as just where prospects of success not reasonably assessed.
- American Cyanamid Co decided in 1975 when
- concerns about pre-trial delays were rising and "interim warfare" was prime cause for delays.
- CPR into effect in 1998 with new approach to case management.
- context within which American Cyanamid principles designed to operate altered significantly.

- Under CPR, early identification and resolution of issues (by application for summary judgment etc.) is encouraged and
- tests according to which early disposal may be achieved are different to previously.

***

31.6 Standard disclosure requires party to disclose only documents– see chapter 13

- on which he relies; and
- which—
- adversely affect own case;
- adversely affect another Ps case; or
- support another P's case; and
- required to disclose by relevant practice direction.

31.16—Disclosure before proceedings start

- rule applies where application for disclosure before proceedings start
- must be supported by evidence.
- court may make order only where—
- R likely P to proceedings;
- A also likely P to those proceedings;
- if proceedings had started, R's of standard disclosure, would extend to docs A seeks disclosure of; and
- disclosure before proceedings start desirable to—
- dispose fairly of anticipated proceedings;
- help dispute to be resolved; or
- save costs.
- order under must—
- specify docs or classes of docs R must disclose; and
- require him, when making disclosure, to specify docs—
- no longer in his control; or
- he claims right or duty to withhold inspection to.
- ➡ order may—
- require R to indicate what happened to docs no longer in his control; and

- specify time and place for disclosure and inspection.

31.17—Orders for disclosure against 3rd party
- rule applies where application for disclosure by person not P proceedings.
- must be supported by evidence.
- court may make order only where—
- docs sought likely to support case of A or adversely affect case of other Ps to proceedings; and
- disclosure necessary to dispose fairly of claim or save costs.
- order must—
- specify docs or classes of docs R must disclose; and
- require R, when making disclosure, to specify docs—
- no longer in his control; or
- he claims right or duty to withhold inspection to.
* order may—
- require R to indicate what happened to docs no longer in his control; and
- specify time and place for disclosure and inspection.

***

52.3—Permission to appeal– see chapter 23
- appellant or respondent requires permission to appeal—
- ..
- application for permission to appeal may be made—
- to lower court - at hearing at which decision appealing made; or
- to appeal court in appeal notice.
- Where lower court refuses permission to appeal—
- further application may be made to appeal court; and
- order refusing permission will specify—
- court to which further application for permission should be made; and
- level of judge who should hear application.
- Subject to para (4A), where appeal court, without hearing, refuses permission to appeal, person seeking permission may request decision be reconsidered at hearing.
- (4A)

- Where judge of Court of Appeal or High Court, refuses permission to appeal without hearing and considers application totally without merit, he may order person seeking permission may not request decision to be reconsidered at hearing.
- ..
• request under (4) must be filed within 7 days after service of notice of permission refused.
• Permission to appeal may be given where—
• appeal has real prospect of success; or
• some other compelling reason appeal should be heard.
(1) An order giving permission may—
(a) limit issues to be heard; and
(b) be made subject to conditions.

***

R v Hayes [1977] 1WLR234 – see chapters 5 and 18

S96 Children's Act
Test for Unsworn evidence for children.
(1) (2) applies where child called as witness in civil proceedings does not, in opinion of court, understand nature of oath.
(2) child's evidence may be heard by court if he, —
1. understands duty to speak the truth; and
2. has sufficient understanding to justify his evidence being heard.
• ...

***

26.6—Tracks– see chapter 12
• **small claims** track normal for—
- any claim for **PI** where—
• value not more than £10,000; and
• claim for damages for PSLA of not more than £1,000;
• any claim by a residential tenant against landlord where—
- tenant seeking order for landlord for repairs or work to premises;
- cost of work estimated at not more than £1,000; and
- value of any other claim for damages not more than £1,000.
• ..

- small claims is normal track for any claim with value of not more than £10,000.
  (Rule 26.7(4) provides court will not allocate to small claims, claims re harassment or unlawful eviction.)
- **fast track** is normal track for any claim—
  * ..
  * with value—
- of not more than £25,000;
- ..
- fast track is normal track for claims in (4) only if court considers—
  * trial likely to be no more than one day; and
  * oral expert evidence will be limited to—
2) 1 expert per P; and
3) expert evidence in 2 fields.
- **multi-track** normal track for any claim for which small claims or fast track not normal track.

***

4+m kwx — chu
Oat HunNice.

19946215R00100